This Book is dedicated to all those who faithfully and continually teach God's Word. Thank you for your consistency year in and year out!

FALLING IN LOVE WITH GOD'S WORD

Mike Sternad

FALLING IN LOVE WITH GOD'S WORD:
A DEVOTIONAL THROUGH PSALM 119

Published by Contented Life Publishing

Calvary Chapel Mobile

Web site: www.calvarychapelmobile.com

Mailing Address: 312 T Schillinger Rd. S, Mobile, Alabama 36608

Phone: 251-287-1253

E-mail: mikesternad@gmail.com

Copyright © 2019 by Mike Sternad

All rights reserved. No part of this publication may be reproduced, stored in a retrieval system, or transmitted in any form or by any means without the express written consent of Mike Sternad.

Unless otherwise indicated, Scripture quotations in this book are taken from the New King James Version of the Bible. Copyright © 1979, 1980, 1982 by Thomas Nelson, Inc., Publishers. Used by permission.

Edited by Miriam Rogers
Cover Design by Ashley Garcia
Interior Design by Ulrika Towgood

Printed in the United States of America

FOREWORD

If you hold your hand on your chest, you'll feel the rhythmic pounding of your heart as it circulates blood through veins and arteries across your body. Your heart, located in a central area of your body, is keeping you alive and healthy.

Similarly, found almost directly at the center of your Bible is a book of Scriptures that provides the heartbeat of God's Word, Psalm 119. It is a treasure trove of truth packed to the brim with promises and power.

The Bible is a miraculous book, written and compiled over 1,500 years by about forty authors living in multiple continents, speaking and writing in different languages. We'll never fully plunge the depths of Scripture, but Psalm 119 is a God-breathed poetic attempt at doing just that.

As you dive into this insightful devotional on Psalm 119 written by Mike Sternad, you'll also find yourself *falling in love with God's Word,* as the title claims. And when you fall in love with God's Word, you'll never be the same!

I hope this devotional creates a unique thirst in your soul that can only be satisfied by God's Word!

Kevin Miller
Lead Pastor, Awaken Church

INTRODUCTION

When I moved from Northern California to Southern California in my early twenties, I had no idea my life would be forever transformed. I was trying to make a name for myself as a musician, and in my mind become somebody that mattered. At the time my search for truth started and I began reading a Bible that someone had purchased for me. I didn't know where to start so I began in the gospel of Matthew. As I read, I found answers to every deep life question I've ever had. I realized then that I held the truth in my hands, and I wanted more.

Soon I began attending Calvary Chapel LAX where the Word of God was taught every single Sunday morning and Wednesday night. There I got saved and hungered to know more about the Lord and I desired to grow in my faith. The more I read the Word of God, the more I learned and the more my heart longed to know the Lord deeper. I was on fire for God and all I wanted to do was to flourish in the faith. I believed reading and meditating upon the Bible was the source of spiritual growth. I loved the Word so much that I wanted to read it, talk about it and teach it. Years after I began attending the church and serving in various ministries, I was ordained as a pastor at Calvary Chapel LAX. Eventually I went on to plant Calvary Chapel Mobile in Alabama, where I currently serve as the pastor. Yet even with all the things God has done and is doing in my life, after all these years, I continue to read God's Word daily because it keeps me close to Him. He speaks to me through His Word, keeping my faith fortified.

God's Word contains the nutrients to not only give us life but to cause our faith to flourish.

I absolutely believe that the Scriptures are the source of spiritual strength and the foundation of our lives as Christians.

My goal and prayer for writing this devotional is that as you read it, you'll fall in love with God's Word and grow in your faith. The Bible is such a critical aspect of your life as a Jesus follower. When you read it, you get to know His heart and will for you. God's Word is His love letter to His children. He speaks to you through the Scriptures. Use the Word in your everyday life as a weapon against the temptations that try and tear you down.

Psalm 119 is the longest chapter in the Bible and it's all about God's Word. Read it, get into it, and let it seep into your heart and affect your life. Fall in love with the Lord's Word and let it transform you into the person God is calling you to be. You won't regret it.

Mike Sternad
Believer, husband, father, pastor (servant)

PSALM 119

1 BLESSED ARE THE UNDEFILED IN THE WAY, WHO WALK IN THE LAW OF THE LORD!

The way to be blessed in this life is to be *undefiled*. The word *undefiled* means "one that is whole, healthy and complete." In our society today, the idea of being pure and walking according to the Spirit, rather than walking in the flesh, is seen as foolish. It is sad how far a society can fall when the Lord is taken out of the equation. Many believe that to be undefiled is boring and dull—that in order to have fun, one has to give in to the lusts they feel. This is not the way to blessings; this is the way to massive burdens. Never let any worldly activities cause defilement to enter into your mind or heart. Be on guard. Watch and pray. Know that the way to be blessed is to live life God's way, not our own way. Don't let defilement deter you from following the Lord.

As long as you are in step with the Lord you will remain undefiled and therefore, you'll be extremely blessed. When you walk in the law of the Lord, you will be blessed in all that you do. Let God's Word permeate your mind and heart so that it can protect you against the possible defilement that stems from the world, the enemy and the flesh. As you read and adhere to God's Word, it will become clear what truth steps you need to take to stay pure. You are not called to be perfect (that's impossible), you are called to be pure. Being pure in heart means living your life fully for the Lord and not engaging in habitual sin. If you mess up, be quick to repent; keep your eyes on the Lord as your heart is surrendered to Him. By staying undefiled and walking with the Lord, adhering to His perfect Word, you will be blessed.

2 BLESSED ARE THOSE WHO KEEP HIS TESTIMONIES, WHO SEEK HIM WITH THE WHOLE HEART!

The word *keep* here doesn't just mean "hearing," it means "doing" His testimonies. It's not enough to think about God's Word; we also need to enact it in our daily lives. Many times we can read a verse in the Bible and be blown away by its power, but then we don't use it in our life situations. God's Word is not meant to sit on a shelf collecting dust, it is meant to be read, digested and lived out. To keep His testimonies, we need to continually dig into God's Word and let it sink deep into our hearts. Reading what the Lord says and getting to know Him through the Scriptures really does lead to joy. To seek God with our whole heart is to be in absolute surrender to Him, His Word and His ways. God doesn't want weekend visits, or occasional meetings, He wants full custody of His children.

I don't want to have a divided heart when it comes to seeking God. He is the One we worship, trust in fully and follow. I am truly blessed when I give up my selfish ways and follow the Lord's plan for me. Seek the Lord with every part of who you are and watch Him meet your life's needs like nothing or no one else can. May it be said of you that you are daily and diligently pursuing your relationship with the Lord as you keep His perfect Word.

3 THEY ALSO DO NO INIQUITY; THEY WALK IN HIS WAYS.

This verse echoes verses one and two. Note that anytime God's Word touches on a truth more than once, it is incredibly important. *Iniquity* means "unrighteousness" and "wickedness." Iniquity should never be an earmark of a follower of Jesus. Yes, we will make mistakes and commit sin; yet, a mark of spiritual maturity is being quick to repent and immediately getting back on track with the Lord.

The point of this verse is that goodness and purity should mark the life of a believer. We can never conjure up goodness from within our own hearts. The good that we possess is given to us from above. As believers we don't follow our own ways, we follow the Lord's ways. Walking in step with God means living to please Him, not ourselves. Walking in God's ways means single-heartedly pursuing God—therefore, letting God annihilate iniquity from our hearts. When I am in step with the ways of the Lord, I feel truly free and relieved! There is no guilt that I'm harboring and I'm not walking through this life feeling condemned. Daily you have the choice to either walk in your own ways or in the Lord's path. One leads to being lost, the other leads to the Lord. Choose wisely.

4 YOU HAVE COMMANDED US TO KEEP YOUR PRECEPTS DILIGENTLY.

The path to being blessed is to be obedient to God's Word. Being obedient is a great blessing, not a burden. As the Lord's commandments are laid out for us to dig into, we will get to know what He wants and walk in His will. When we act on His Word, it brings joy to our hearts and freedom that this world can't provide. Keeping God's precepts helps us stay on the path of God's purposes.

Not only are we to *keep* God's Word but do it diligently. This means we are to go to great lengths and degrees to do what must be done to stay on the track of God's ways. Sometimes we may have to cut off relationships, drastically change bad habits, or even rearrange our daily routines. God's Word isn't a moral book we simply stick in our minds; it is God's voice to us, His people.

My personal testimony is that my way didn't work. My way led to a wilderness experience where I was lost with no one and nothing to hold on to. When I got saved and started to dig into God's decrees, the direction for my life became clear. Since then I've wanted to do what I must to make sure I am staying in God's Word and adhering to God's ways daily. It's so critical for the health of our spiritual lives to do this because it is what sets us apart from the *wilderness* called the world.

5 OH, THAT MY WAYS WERE DIRECTED TO KEEP YOUR STATUTES!

We have to realize and remember that we cannot keep God's statutes apart from His work in us. Without God's help, we lack the ability, wisdom and strength to obey His Word. The Lord directs us, and then enables and equips us to follow in His ways. Apart from the Lord's enabling, we really cannot do anything of value. The Lord grants us all we need to conquer those forces that bring discouragement and doubt. When I realized that God's Word is a weapon, I began using it to fight off temptation and to direct my life choices. The result was gaining clarity for my everyday life.

May your heart be settled as you follow God's statutes with the strength that He blesses you with. Let Him direct your every step, your every situation and circumstance. He knows what you need and He knows what He is doing. Let God guide you by His Word through every decision that you are called to make in this world.

6 THEN I WOULD NOT BE ASHAMED, WHEN I LOOK INTO ALL YOUR COMMANDMENTS.

If our ways are directed by God's Word, then we will not be ashamed of the way we are living our lives. We are not called to perfection, which is impossible, we are called to look into God's perfect Word for divine direction. As long as we are hungering for the Lord and peering into His precepts, we are secure by being in the source of His will. The Bible is God-breathed; it is our navigation system for every area of life. The Word of God is never outdated. Don't be ashamed of what His Word says—believe in it and live it out. Don't just read the Bible, do what it says.

It is such a great reminder for me that I never have to be ashamed of what the Lord says. My life is based upon and established by God's Word and I never want that to change. I love the words that the Lord speaks to me as I open the Bible and pray for clarity. Every single truth that is contained in His commandments are food for our souls. The Scriptures contain the spiritual nutrients that we ingest and grow from. Dig into His

Word unashamedly and live out what God has laid out for you in His commandments.

7 I WILL PRAISE YOU WITH UPRIGHTNESS OF HEART, WHEN I LEARN YOUR RIGHTEOUS JUDGMENTS.

God is a just judge and His Word is the measuring rod by which we live. When we learn of the Lord's ways, they truly cause praise to flow from our hearts and lives. Not only does reading the Bible result in spiritual growth for our souls, the Bible lifts our countenance and gives us confidence in Christ. We can walk confidently in Him because as we adhere to His Word, we realize that we are completely free. The guilt is gone; replaced with an awareness of His amazing forgiveness.

The idea behind the word *uprightness* is "to do what is right and acceptable." In this case, what is right is doing what God has laid out in His Word. I love that we can freely praise God because of His Word spoken to us. It brings such joy knowing that the Lord has given us the Bible to soak in and live out. I love to meditate upon the Word of the Lord in the mornings because it lifts my countenance and prepares me for the day ahead. God's Word really gets my mind and heart prepared. It encourages me and sets the tone for every future situation.

Praise God today for the Scriptures He has blessed you with. You have the privilege of starting every day in God's Word and taking His truth personally. When you learn the truths of God, you will confidently praise God for who He is and what He has done in your life.

8 I WILL KEEP YOUR STATUTES; OH, DO NOT FORSAKE ME UTTERLY!

The word *keep* in this verse is the notion of "guarding." God's Word truly guards our hearts and protects us from the daily temptations we face. *Statutes* means "the engraved or written Word of God." I love that as we read God's Word, it becomes ingrained and burned in our hearts. It seems that the psalmist was pretty desperate in his plea not to be forsaken by God. But those of us who have an active relationship with the Lord know how a heart desperate for God is a good thing because it demonstrates our total dependence on Him and Him alone. As the Bible clearly states, the Lord is with us always, wherever we go (Joshua 1:9).

There have been countless times that I've felt alone in this world. Yet, as I seek the Lord in prayer and through His Word, I remember and realize once again that God is with me every minute of every day, bringing comfort to my heart that no human can give. You can find comfort in the fact that God is with you and will never leave you. If you feel far from God, it is not He who moved—you did. Your heart will be settled and at rest when you draw near to God. James 4:8 says, "Draw near to God and He will draw near to you."

9 HOW CAN A YOUNG MAN CLEANSE HIS WAY? BY TAKING HEED ACCORDING TO YOUR WORD.

This verse tells us it is important from a young age to deal with habitual sin in order to keep from being in bondage to sin later on. In a sense, when a believer is young, he is setting the tone for the rest of his life. Taking heed to the Scriptures is the way to cleanse a young man's way. God's wisdom will keep you from walking in lewd and ungodly ways; while teaching you to be proactive in seeking the almighty God through His statutes.

Anytime I just let things happen, I end up drifting away from the Lord and His ways. I have learned that I cannot be passive in my Christian walk or I will get pummeled by the ungodly influences that surround me. When I'm proactive, I'm well-prepared and equipped by God to fight the forces of the enemy.

You are saved and called to pursue the Lord, to foster your spiritual life and forge ahead in the faith. As you read God's Word, you'll realize the blessedness of purity. If your way needs to be cleansed, cling to God's Word, follow the Lord with your entire being, and the result will be walking in purity.

10 WITH MY WHOLE HEART I HAVE SOUGHT YOU; OH, LET ME NOT WANDER FROM YOUR COMMANDMENTS!

The idea here is that the believer would be completely committed to pursuing the Lord. When we commit our whole heart to God, it shows a level of commitment that is unparalleled. In the same verse, the psalmist notes his proclivity to wander from the Word of the Lord. It doesn't take long for us to wander away from the Lord when we wander far from His Word. If we stop our digging into the Scriptures, then it will result in drifting away from God's ways.

When I was a new believer, there was a time where I drifted from God's decrees, and therefore I was out of fellowship with Him. I didn't want to get into the Bible because I was into the things of the world. I was lost and confused, and far from where God wanted me to be. It wasn't until I got back into His Word that I began to be in line with His will. What I remember vividly is how good it was to be in the Scriptures again and closely connected to the Lord.

May your heart continually seek the Lord fully and completely. May you not wander away from God but pursue His heart. Keep focused on the One who formed and fashioned you. He loves you and wants a heart that fully falls upon Him. Surrendering to the Lord will halt wandering and bring about heartfelt worship that will keep you close to God.

11 YOUR WORD I HAVE HIDDEN IN MY HEART, THAT I MIGHT NOT SIN AGAINST YOU.

As believers, when we are in habitual sin we live contrary to God's design. So what is the key to resist the temptations we face? God's Word is the answer. The word *hidden* in this verse means "treasure." I love that the Scripture truly is a treasure we can cherish and cling to for divine protection from habitual sin. When we hide the Word in our hearts, we are letting the truth seep into the core of who we are. *Heart* here means the inner part of who you are. So as we read and take in God's Word, we hide it like treasure in our hearts and when we need it the most, we bring it to the surface and use it to fend off the enemy's attacks.

I can't tell you how many times I've used God's Word as a weapon to fight off temptation. But the only way I can use God's Word is to first have it in the holster of my heart. The more I regularly read the Scriptures, the more I am prepared for the daily battle I face as a believer. If you are faced with a recurring temptation, open the treasure chest of the Scriptures and use them to resist sin and fight for the faith. Hide His Word in your heart and ask God to reveal those specific Scriptures that will guard you when temptation tests you.

12 BLESSED ARE YOU, O LORD! TEACH ME YOUR STATUTES.

Praising God is an action that will set our hearts aflame. As we worship Him, we prepare our hearts to receive His Word into our lives. When we get into the Scriptures, a great habit is to pray before we read, as we read, and after we read. Personally, I don't want to look at the Bible like a textbook where I simply memorize the words and recite them on command. I want to hear the Lord speaking to me through His truth. God's statutes are the avenue by which He speaks to us. Seek God and pray even as you are reading the Bible and you will be pleasantly surprised. Ask the Lord to teach you what you need to learn in this life and specifically for every situation. God is always speaking to you through His Word. The question is, are you listening?

13 WITH MY LIPS I HAVE DECLARED ALL THE JUDGMENTS OF YOUR MOUTH.

We not only have the privilege of reading God's Word; we have ample opportunities to declare it as well. Taking in the Scriptures without ever giving them out will lead to a spiritual life that is lethargic. In order to keep the Word alive in our lives, we must share it with the world. The Bible is not meant to be ingrained in our hearts only to forever stay there. We need to share the Word because when we do, it truly ignites our passion for the Lord. We do not declare our opinions or views on life, we declare God's truth and His view.

We are meant to take in God's decrees and then give them out. When I read the Word and share what I've read, a fire ignites in my heart and all I want to do is share more! As the Lord's words affect your heart, it's exciting to share what the Lord has spoken to you. Declare His Word and the result will be a fire in your heart that will prod you to declare it even more.

14 I HAVE REJOICED IN THE WAY OF YOUR TESTIMONIES, AS MUCH AS IN ALL RICHES.

Riches do not and will never bring a fullness and satisfaction to a life. Yet, the concept of riches really excites many people. What is truly satisfying is reading God's Word because the result is a passion to pursue God more. His Word is worth more than all the treasure on this earth. As we get to know God's ways through His Word, as the Scriptures proclaim about salvation and eternal matters, we realize its truth is what we treasure. The truth sets us free—the truth gives us a glimpse of the Lord's heart—and it gives us cause for rejoicing. When I read the Bible, it truly brings up joy and passion in my heart.

I am constantly in awe of the riches I find in the Bible; it's a book to be read and a treasure to be used. We are rich spiritually and we can access those riches every day of the week when we open the treasure of God's Word. Watch your faith flourish and your spiritual life soar as you grow exponentially in eternal matters.

15   I WILL MEDITATE ON YOUR PRECEPTS, AND CONTEMPLATE YOUR WAYS.

To meditate means to ponder. The things we think about are usually ruminations of things we truly care about. When one contemplates the commandments of the Lord, what becomes clear is the fact that God's promises are sure. His precepts are perfect and pondering over them throughout the day does our heart good.

When I read the promises of God, I don't want to soon forget them. I want to think about them, meditate on what His Word says, and reflect on how God is actually speaking to me. If I am pondering God's Word in my heart from my morning devotion, I am spiritually aware throughout the day. The Word percolates in my mind and consistently speaks to my heart. When you contemplate the precepts of the Lord, you think about what God is saying to you. This healthy spiritual habit will help you stay on the track of God's will. It will help you to keep in line with His precepts and purposes. Meditate upon His Word on a daily basis and take heed as your calling becomes completely clear.

16   I WILL DELIGHT MYSELF IN YOUR STATUTES; I WILL NOT FORGET YOUR WORD.

In this verse, *delight* connotes the action of "jumping for joy." The word is emphatic and truly gives a picture of the amazing effect of digging into the decrees of God. If you want to be joyful and delighted, spend time hearing God's voice within His statutes. The word *statutes* has to do with something that is prescribed. No matter what situational dilemma you may find yourself in, know that the prescription to help you out is God's perfect Word. The more you seek God through the Scriptures, the less likely you will be to forget what you've read. Ironically, we often forget what we should remember and remember what we should forget.

I don't want to forget what God has said to me. I want to remember His words that met me in my present trial. I want to delight in the verses God brought to my mind when life seemed muddled and mundane. I want to have triumph over my trial because of the words God had spoken to me as I went through a similar situation in the past. Remember God's statutes by staying in them. Find your delight in hearing God's voice to your very life as you meditate upon His Word.

17 DEAL BOUNTIFULLY WITH YOUR SERVANT, THAT I MAY LIVE AND KEEP YOUR WORD.

This verse makes it clear that we can both ask for blessings and, at the same time, be totally dependent upon the Lord. God blesses us more than we know. He provides every spiritual blessing and gives us the strength we need to keep His perfect Word. We can make requests of Him and He directs our lives. Sometimes we don't pray to the Lord because we assume He will not answer our prayers. Remember that the Lord loves to bless His children. We can come boldly to God in expectation that He will deal well with us and answer our prayers, no matter how "big."

I love to pray for things that seem impossible because the Lord is fully capable of answering those prayers. I don't want to limit God by only praying for small things.

I know that God is limitless and can do the impossible. Pray with faith knowing that God can do some heart-altering, life-transforming work. Your life is to be lived to seek Him with your whole heart, keeping His Word. As you daily ponder God's precepts, the results are answered prayer and abundant blessings. If you feel like you are never blessed, then I encourage you to open up the Bible and seek His will. Don't let anything hinder your reading of God's Word; allow the Lord to equip you with all you need to not only survive but to spiritually thrive.

18 OPEN MY EYES, THAT I MAY SEE WONDROUS THINGS FROM YOUR LAW.

For the person who is saved, the spiritual aspects of life become clear. Before I met Christ, I read God's Word and was incredibly intrigued by it. After I was saved, a transparency of eternity enlightened my life. I was able to read God's Word and actually understand what it meant in the context of my personal life. My eyes were opened, and I was in awe of how God marvelously communicated to me through the words that I read. What used to be ordinary became amazing. What I excused as everyday occurrences became divine appointments. I fell more and more in love with the Lord as I dug deeper and deeper into His Word. Believers are to be lifelong students of the Scriptures and we should always be learning from Him. Continue to read the words of the Lord and expect direction from the One who paves your path and directs your steps. As you pursue Him, your spiritual eyes will be opened and your life's purpose will be illuminated. As you continue to open up God's Word, may He continue to open your eyes to the mighty life He has called you to.

19 I AM A STRANGER IN THE EARTH; DO NOT HIDE YOUR COMMANDMENTS FROM ME.

The psalmist is clear—he does not fit into this fallen world. We are pilgrims and sojourners on this earth and we are simply passing through. If you feel like you fit in perfectly with this world, then you may not be living fully for the Lord. Not fitting into the trends of the culture means that we are on the right track. The fact is, we as believers stand out in this world that seems to be sinking deeper and deeper into depravity. People have looked at me like I was so strange when they realize I am a Christian and I'm not ashamed of it. I know my time on earth is limited, so I do not wish to waste time on stuff that makes no eternal impact. I want to daily live for the Lord as if it were my last day of life.

As the darkness continues to spread throughout this world, we are blessed to shine the light of Christ, telling truth as we are engaging with the lost, helpless and hopeless. We are messengers of the news that can break people out of the mold of carnal conformity. People need the Scriptures to feed on spiritually as much as they need food to nourish them physically.

Don't hold too tightly to things of this earth but hold onto the Lord as He uses you mightily during your short time here. You were made for much more than simply attempting to be comfortable on this earth and making your home here. Remember that you only have so much time on this earth. Life flies by quickly, so have a sense of urgency when it comes to spiritual truth. Know that your true home is not here but in heaven.

20 MY SOUL BREAKS WITH LONGING FOR YOUR JUDGMENTS AT ALL TIMES.

The psalmist longed for God's Word because he was a stranger in the land. When we are sojourners in this world, we realize that nothing on earth truly satisfies our souls. We spiritually starve without God's Word. Our soul is fed when our diet consists of nothing but the Scriptures. The word *judgments* in this verse means "God's Word." So as we see this world crumbling beneath us, we know that the Word grants us insight into the spiritual realm and gives us a glimpse of our glorious future. When I periodically read God's Word, this world beats me up—but God's Word builds me up. I not only desire to be in the Word, I need to be in the Word. God has written out the right way to live a righteous and blameless life. I simply need to read it and heed it.

May you feed off of the Bible so as to be filled with a hope that is sure and a confidence that stems from your Creator. You have the great opportunity to daily focus upon God's Word to get your perspective pointed toward what matters in this life. Fill your soul!

21 YOU REBUKE THE PROUD—THE CURSED, WHO STRAY FROM YOUR COMMANDMENTS.

Those who are proud want nothing to do with God and they demonstrate this by their lack of adherence to His ways. God rebukes those who run in the opposite direction from Him, who stray from His ways. Nothing good can ever come from disobedience; being astray from God's ways is a horrible place to be in.

Thankfully, God rebukes those who fail to listen. A rebuke from the Lord will often lead a person back on track with Him. Honestly I can say that I love when the Scriptures I'm reading rebuke an action I've taken or an attitude I have. I welcome rebukes from the Lord because it is in those times where I realize I need to cling to God deeply and desperately. As the Lord points out things in our lives that are not of Him, we can repent and receive forgiveness.

You are blessed when you walk closely with God. Cling to Him so as not to fall away or go astray on a path without purpose. If you are in sin or walking the line and flirting with ungodly things, God will point that out. It's up to you to repent of those things and find forgiveness in the Lord who doesn't condone your sin, but He doesn't condemn you either. He simply wants you to come clean and repent so that you can be fully restored and back on track with Him.

22 REMOVE FROM ME REPROACH AND CONTEMPT, FOR I HAVE KEPT YOUR TESTIMONIES.

There are those who reproach us for digging into God's Word. *Reproach* is when people "disapprove" of something we are doing. *Contempt* in this context means we are "thought of as worthless and useless" because we read God's Word. Why are some people so harsh toward us for believing absolute truth? Why the animosity and hate? Many unbelievers hate that we read God's Word because they know that they aren't living how God desires them to live. Out of guilt they put a guilt trip on us for being in the Bible and actually doing what it says. Yet, instead of praying against these people, may we pray for them. They need to get right with the Lord, and we have the truth that can infiltrate their hearts of hate with God's perfect love.

I've had people argue with me about the faith until they were blue in the face. They aren't open to listening; they just want to make their point and win the debate. Yet, I don't want to give up on them; I pray for them because they are lost. People will come against you for the faith you have in God's Word and God's ways. They will not like that you absolutely love the Lord. Even still, be a light and reflect God's love to those people who have so much hate in their hearts toward the faith. Never stop praying for them. God is more than capable of transforming them from unbelievers to Bible-believing Christians.

23 PRINCES ALSO SIT AND SPEAK AGAINST ME, BUT YOUR SERVANT MEDITATES ON YOUR STATUTES.

People in authority were against the psalmist for meditating on God's Word, but he did not let that stop him. As believers, the absolute authority that we follow is God's Word, not man's ways. In the face of adversity, we still bury our noses in the Scriptures as they truly bring life and truth to our minds and hearts. We are God's servants who peer into His guidebook to know why we serve Him and how to serve Him.

Without the guidance of God's Word, I would not know what is going on in my own life! His Word has directed me to serve in many ministries and reach out in different ways. I would never have moved my family across the country and planted a church 2,000 miles away without meditating upon His Word first. I don't want to guess at big life decisions. I want to meditate on God's Word and get my directives from the One I am dependent on.

You have the privilege of meditating on the precepts of our God. You get to pray in His Word so that you will be soul satisfied and set on the right path. You can dig into the Scriptures on a daily basis and grow like crazy as you let the Word soak into your soul. Take it in and water your heart with God's Word.

24 YOUR TESTIMONIES ALSO ARE MY DELIGHT AND MY COUNSELORS.

The truth in God's Word brings such counsel to our daily lives. What a delight to hear of God's heart as we simply read the books of the Bible. The psalmist delighted in the Word of God more than in the princes and authorities on the earth. The Lord truly has the authority—He is the authority I adhere to; my delight. I absolutely love reading the Bible and knowing God's truth is washing over me and leading me to a deeper, more profound relationship with Him. Following God is the greatest privilege and blessing in my life. His Word is my counsel in all of my circumstances and situations. I go to God's counsel before I ever go to any human counsel.

The Lord knows what you need to hear and He speaks to you from His Word. The Scriptures counsel you on the way to live, how to live and why you live. What a joy! Get into God's Word and let it get into your heart, filling you with abundant joy.

25 MY SOUL CLINGS TO THE DUST; REVIVE ME ACCORDING TO YOUR WORD.

The psalmist was at a low place of despair. The word *dust* in the Scriptures means "a place of death." His soul felt dead, but the beautiful thing about his despair was the prayer immediately after it. He asked for a revived heart. When we are feeling spiritually dry or even spiritually dead, it's time to cry out to the Lord who can refresh and reboot our spiritual system. According to this psalm, the key ingredient for a revived heart is God's Word. We need to quit clinging to dead things and start clinging to the Lord's living Word. Feed your soul with the Scriptures and the result will be a revived heart that changes from dry to alive. Before I was saved, my heart was sunk spiritually and I had no clue about new life in Christ. I was lost and alone with no hope and no help. When I began reading the Word, my heart came alive and I truly realized the power that comes from reading God's precepts. Let the Bible bombard your life and let it water your soul with revival. Whether you are on the mountaintop or in the valley, don't neglect the saturation of your soul with the Scriptures. It will make all the difference in your mind, heart and life.

26 I HAVE DECLARED MY WAYS, AND YOU ANSWERED ME; TEACH ME YOUR STATUTES.

This verse makes it clear that the psalmist was fully open and honest with the Lord. He shared everything with Him through prayer. We can seek God with a heart that is completely transparent, and He will not turn us away. Be honest with Him. As you are an open book before the Lord, He will listen, and the answers will come. God is faithful to answer the pleas of His people.

There have been times where I desperately called out to the Lord in complete honesty and He didn't strike me down! Instead, God listened and answered me and gave me confirmation from His Word. Over and over I have seen that God is so incredibly faithful. He will answer you as you call out to Him for wisdom. Don't be afraid to share everything with the Lord. Even though He already knows what you're going through, God wants you to share with Him all that is in your heart. Be honest with the Lord and open your heart. As you search the Scriptures, be prepared to be taught the absolute truth into your life.

27 MAKE ME UNDERSTAND THE WAY OF YOUR PRECEPTS; SO SHALL I MEDITATE ON YOUR WONDERFUL WORKS.

Not only do we need knowledge of God's Word, we need understanding as well. To get deep spiritual understanding of what the Lord's Word means, we need to ask Him for that understanding. And when we understand something, we will take action on that understanding. The more I am spoken to from the Word of God, the more I want to share with others what God has personally spoken to me. I love to take one verse, like this devotional, mull it over all day long, think about it, pray about it, and use it in my life. I believe one of God's most wonderful works is the Bible. His Word will work in your heart and continue to transform your life. May you peer into God's precepts daily and seek to gain knowledge of His Word. Seek to understand it so you can be effective in sharing what He's teaching you. Make God's precepts a priority in your everyday life and watch God work.

28 MY SOUL MELTS FROM HEAVINESS; STRENGTHEN ME ACCORDING TO YOUR WORD.

The psalmist lacked strength and the freedom that emanates from following the Lord. Whatever hardship he faced, it affected his soul and burdened his heart. There are trials we go through that are deep and dark and seem to last forever. Sometimes it would seem like there is no way for us to get out of the tribulation that so intensely weighs us down. What better time to passionately cry out to the Lord in honesty and dependency. There are moments we feel so weak that getting through the day seems impossible.

I have been at my wit's end time and time again. I have been burnt out and discouraged. I've dealt with difficulties that wearied me to the point of giving up. Each time I got in these lulls, I cried out to the Lord in desperation and He met me right in the middle of my discouraging moment. I can depend upon the Lord every day of my life. Cry out to the Lord and He will be your strength in your state of weakness. God will give you endurance and perseverance to get through each difficult day. Being a child of God means the Lord loves to lavish you with all you need to get through tough times and come out with a smile.

29 REMOVE FROM ME THE WAY OF LYING, AND GRANT ME YOUR LAW GRACIOUSLY.

The psalmist was conscious of his own tendency to lie even though he knew he needed to adhere to the truth of God's Word. Every day we have the choice to live for truth or be caught up in lies. When we speak lies, we are really lying to and sinning against the Lord. If there is repetitive sin in our lives that we want conquered, the way to overcome is to ask the Lord for strength to put the sin behind us. He has the power to pummel the sin that so easily affects us, and the ones we love. I've struggled with sins that seem to never leave me alone. The enemy, the world, and the flesh work together to cause me to fail and fall away from the faith. What I've learned over and over again is that God is stronger than every sin that I've struggled with. God's power in my life will guard against the lures that surround me. As I'm seeking Him through His Word, I then use the Scriptures to gain victory over every vicious temptation that I face. When you are in the law of the Lord (the Bible), the truth penetrates your heart and your actions will follow. Whatever sin you may be struggling with, when you stay connected to God's Word, you are less likely to wander away from Him. Stay in the truth and ask God to remove lying— or anything that is not of Him—from your life. When you are willing to be proactive in the truth, God is faithful to cleanse you from those besetting sins.

30 I HAVE CHOSEN THE WAY OF TRUTH; YOUR JUDGMENTS I HAVE LAID BEFORE ME.

The psalmist was able to choose the way of truth because he was in the truth on a regular basis. What we're focused on is what we'll live by. So if we are focused on the things of the world, we will follow the trends of the world. If we are focused on God's Word, then we will put in place those spiritual principles that will help us progress in our walk with the Lord. I've seen one too many Christians who were unsteady in their walk with the Lord because they were inconsistent in their devotion lives.

When I get out of the habit of daily digging into God's Word, I stop thinking of the spiritual realm and begin focusing on what I can see. As a believer I need to realize and remember that I'm living for more than what's on the surface. I'm living to please the Lord, accomplish His purposes, and daily walk with Him. He is the meaning of life! Every truth that I hold onto is contained in the Bible.

When you place God's Word before you on a daily basis, you are setting the tone for the rest of your day. Your perspective will be in line with pleasing the Lord, and as you focus on God first, then you will place Him foremost throughout the day. May you lay His judgments before you on a regular basis so that a spiritual awareness is on the forefront of your mind. He is why you are here and His will is what you are called to accomplish.

31 I CLING TO YOUR TESTIMONIES; O LORD, DO NOT PUT ME TO SHAME!

When we cling to God's testimonies, there is no way we can be put to shame. Instead, we can openly honor the Lord and boast in His ways. The psalmist was making it clear that he held onto God's Word for dear life because it's what brings life. There is no shame in reading, believing, and enacting God's Word.

Being a new believer years ago, I didn't care what people thought about me reading my Bible in public; I just opened it and dug in. But the longer I was a believer, the more aware I became of what others thought. I began to be timid, especially living in Los Angeles, to bring my Bible out to a coffee shop and read. Then I began praying against passivity and I asked God to annihilate my inhibitions. He answered my prayer and gave me boldness to publicly shine as a light for Him.

It is a privilege and a blessing to base your life upon the Scriptures that God has given you. Cling to the Word with all of who you are and let it shape who you would become. The Word is what washes you and leads you to a healthy repentance and a radical refinement. As you obey what it says, you will be unashamedly blessed.

32 I WILL RUN THE COURSE OF YOUR COMMANDMENTS, FOR YOU SHALL ENLARGE MY HEART.

In the preceding verses, we see a progression as the psalmist went from confessing to choosing to clinging to running. Notice that he is actually putting effort into seeking the Lord by reading His Word. The psalmist is not striving but is simply seeking and pursuing direction from the Lord through the Scriptures. As he was in the Lord's Word, his heart was enlarged. In other words, as we get into God's Word and it's ingrained into our hearts, our spiritual lives grow.

The things of this life constantly fight against my time with the Lord. Distractions, busyness and to-do lists can tend to crowd out my time with the Lord. I've made excuses as to why I can't get into God's Word and spend time seeking Him. Yet, if I am to seek first His kingdom and draw near to Him, then the top of my to-do list every day needs to say, "Seek the Lord!" The more I seek Him, the more He teaches me, speaks to me, and grows my faith.

The spectrum of light that emanates from God's Word shines brighter as you stay in the Bible on a regular basis—then your heart begins to desire what God desires. Read God's Word and watch as the Lord expands your heart for Him and for His people.

33 TEACH ME, O LORD, THE WAY OF YOUR STATUTES, AND I SHALL KEEP IT TO THE END.

Without God it would be impossible to have the strength, wisdom and resolve to keep the statutes of the Lord. We need to depend upon the Lord to enable us to keep His law and His ways. As we read His Word, we should be praying for the Lord to teach us His truth. We are blessed to not only dig into the Scriptures but to pray them in as well.

When I'm doing my devotion time in the mornings, I seek the Lord in prayer at the same time. When I ask the Lord to speak to me through His Word, He does. The Scriptures are living and active, and when I'm expecting the Lord to speak to me, He meets me where I'm at.

As you're reading you can simply ask the Lord to meet you in your life situation and you can be sure He will use His Word to speak directly to you. How amazing is that truth! You can hear and heed the Scriptures when you have a life that is 100 percent dependent upon the Lord. He'll give you all you need to follow His ways. Make it a healthy spiritual habit to dig into God's decrees on a regular basis. You'll never regret it.

34 GIVE ME UNDERSTANDING, AND I SHALL KEEP YOUR LAW; INDEED, I SHALL OBSERVE IT WITH MY WHOLE HEART.

In order for us to fulfill God's will, we need to seek to understand His law. May we not be afraid to admit that we don't have it all together and we cannot know of eternal things apart from the Lord's Word. The Bible is not just a book that we casually read and memorize. The Bible is the basis for all we know to be right and true.

We are blessed to observe it and follow through with what is written in it. We don't get to pick and choose what we believe and not believe. We either believe the whole Word or we don't believe any of it. The whole Bible causes the believer to live in a godly way because it is the whole counsel of God, authored by God. May we not be cafeteria Christians, picking and choosing what we want to believe.

I've been so saddened to see preachers cherry-pick the Bible verses they feel like sharing, instead of going through the whole Word of God. They'll leave out parts of the Bible they disagree with or they'll skew the verses they think are offensive. I want the whole counsel of God so that I can be a well-rounded Bible-based believer.

The more you read God's Word, the more you'll glean God's attributes and live a life according to His heart. You are not called to be self-centered; you are called to be God-centered. The way to place God at the center of your life is by putting the Word before you on a regular basis.

35 MAKE ME WALK IN THE PATH OF YOUR COMMANDMENTS, FOR I DELIGHT IN IT.

The psalmist's plea is to walk in the path God has purposed for him. Without the Lord we can do nothing of eternal meaning. Without the Lord's empowering we are the weakest people on this earth. But with the Lord, we can gain the strength we need to stick to the Scriptures and live out the calling He has for us. When we realize that life change happens when we lean upon the Lord and follow His Word, it revolutionizes our walk with Him.

It is a great blessing to be able to run my race on the track God has laid out for me. The road of His will may not always be smooth, but every step is an adventure. It's exciting to follow the Lord. I would not trade following the Lord for anything in this world.

Seek Him and pursue His great plan for you. Walk in the path of His amazing and grace-filled commandments. Delight in His decrees as you delve into the truth that has set you free. Enjoy living for eternal purposes and revel in the fact that you have His Word to learn from, grow from, and guide your every step.

36 INCLINE MY HEART TO YOUR TESTIMONIES, AND NOT TO COVETOUSNESS.

Pursuing selfish gain is what covetousness leads to. The psalmist understood that God's testimonies and our inclination for self-centered living cannot coincide. When we fix our eyes upon the Lord, we will be satisfied with what He has blessed us with. When we place our eyes upon the world, we will lose focus on the gifts God has provided for us. Our hearts cannot be divided between the things of the Lord and the things of the world. We are either for the Lord and His Word, or we are not. As we read God's Word it reminds us how we are richly blessed with all that we need and more. When we delve into the Scriptures daily, our souls are deeply satisfied.

The fact is, when I start wanting what other people have, I forget how incredibly content I am with what the Lord has blessed me with. Anytime I place heightened value on material things I attempt to find satisfaction in those things—only to be left unsatisfied.

May your heart be full knowing that the Lord fills the gaps in your life and He satisfies the longing of your soul. Don't look at what others have and covet after those things. Look to the Lord and learn to be content with what you already have. The Lord is enough. Anything above and beyond Him is just extra blessings.

37 TURN AWAY MY EYES FROM LOOKING AT WORTHLESS THINGS, AND REVIVE ME IN YOUR WAY.

In this distraction-filled world, how often do we focus on worthless things? Back in the psalmist's day, just like now there were useless things that caused them to get sidetracked and sidelined from living for the Lord. Our hearts can grow dull with carnal and fleshly activities. When we become distracted with things that lure us away from the spiritual, God can redirect our eyes from the earthly to the eternal. The way to go from drifting to being dedicated is to turn our eyes back to God's Word. When you're in the Bible and your heart is receptive to His words, revival begins as God speaks to you and works in you. When your heart is on fire for the Lord, it will burn for all to see and you will truly be a light shining for the Lord. It all starts with God's Word.

38 ESTABLISH YOUR WORD TO YOUR SERVANT, WHO IS DEVOTED TO FEARING YOU.

God's Word can change our hearts and minds. It establishes the truth in our soul so that we can stand on a solid foundation. As we read the Word, it inspires us to be in awe of the Lord and His amazing ways. To fear God means to be astounded at who He is and what He's done. It means giving Him reverence as we realize the privilege of serving Him. To be devoted to fearing God is to see God in light of who we are. He is perfect and so we look to the perfect One in total adoration. We are His faulty kids whom He has filled with faith in order that we can be faithful to His calling.

I started serving by sweeping leaves off the front entrance of our church before service. God kept giving me more ways to serve and I kept saying yes. When we are faithful in the small things, God will bless us with more. We were made to worship the Lord. We were created to seek God through prayer and His Word, and when we do it results in deep devotion to the Lord and His ways. Be established for eternity by dedicating your entire life for the sake of the gospel. Every moment lived for eternity is time not wasted.

39 TURN AWAY MY REPROACH WHICH I DREAD, FOR YOUR JUDGMENTS ARE GOOD.

Reproach means "disgrace." The psalmist is saying that he faces disgrace for being a faithful follower of the Lord. Yet, even with the pushback from people who disagree with God's truth, we can rest on the fact that God is the just judge. When dealing with God-haters we can have rest and reassurance that ultimately God's judgments are completely fair.

The apostle Paul even took pleasure in people coming against him because he knew he was suffering for the sake of the gospel. We don't ask for conflict from God-haters, but when it comes it is a sign that we are living fully for the Lord. There is no need to quiet the truth that emanates from our hearts and mouths. I've had people yell at me and mock me because I believe in the Bible. But I never let those moments pull me down because I have no doubt that God's Word is truth.

We are not judges on this earth; we are truth-tellers living out what the Bible says. We are called to stand upon the truth and not be afraid to tell the truth. Don't let anything stop you from taking in and giving out God's Word. You have the truth to live out through your actions. You can speak out the truth with the power of God. Today's the day.

40 BEHOLD, I LONG FOR YOUR PRECEPTS; REVIVE ME IN YOUR RIGHTEOUSNESS.

To long for something means to desire it. The psalmist longed for God's Word because he knew it leads to a revival in righteousness. The writer knew that if he stayed consistent in God's perfect Word, he would live the way God wanted him to live. We wouldn't know what God actually wanted unless we were immersed in the Word. The Lord clearly lays out why we're alive, how we're to live while on this earth, and what happens when we die. The Bible is clear on all the deep subjects that humanity is curious about. May we acknowledge and realize that God's precepts can penetrate our rocky heart to the point of radical revival.

I like diving into God's decrees because when I do, my attitude is altered and my heart is softened. The Bible gives me God's perspective on every practical aspect of life. And when I have God's perspective I start to see things with a heavenly, rather than a carnal, view. Get into His Word on a daily basis. Long for it. Fall in love with it. Make it a consistent spiritual habit to peer into God's precepts and watch God work in your heart so that His righteousness comes alive in your life.

41 LET YOUR MERCIES COME ALSO TO ME, O LORD —YOUR SALVATION ACCORDING TO YOUR WORD.

The beautiful thing about God's Word is that it brings mercy and salvation. The word *mercies* is plural; the connotation is that mercy is piled upon mercy. God does not lay upon us all the bad things we deserve for being sinners from birth. Instead He lavishes love upon us even while we mess up and stray from His ways. His mercies are freeing and relieving, giving comfort when we feel completely condemned. Even while we were deep in our sin God stepped in and saved us.

There is nothing more glorious than being saved and secured for heaven. It humbles me to know that in the midst of my mess, the Lord still loved me and saved me—and He still loves me. God's mercies are fresh when I wake up every morning. I don't have to condemn myself for past actions because the Lord's mercy makes my sin void. I am overwhelmed when I think of the mercy of God because it really reflects His heart of love for me.

If you feel condemned today, remember God's mercy is always there. His mercy is new every morning. Soak in the mercy of God and remember that He loves you at your worst. He saved you when you were sick with sin. God loves you so much He won't give up on you. That's the miracle of God's mercy.

42 SO SHALL I HAVE AN ANSWER FOR HIM WHO REPROACHES ME, FOR I TRUST IN YOUR WORD.

We seek to please God, not man. We don't live for the praises of people; we live to praise the Lord. People may disapprove of how we are living and who we are living for, but that should not put to halt our trust in God's Word. We know and believe that what God says stands now and forever.

For those who disapprove with how I live according to God's Word, I know I can stand confident in what God's Word says. I don't trust in man's opinions; I trust in God's Word. I've been asked questions about the Lord when I did not feel like answering. Yet, every time the Lord brings verses to my mind and words to my mouth to answer the toughest of questions.

Be ready to answer skeptics and people who disagree with you by always having God's Word in your heart. Dig into the decrees of the Lord and use them to shed light on the hearts that are dim and depressed. Trust in God's Word and speak it out when the Lord brings an opportunity. Be confident in Him.

43 AND TAKE NOT THE WORD OF TRUTH UTTERLY OUT OF MY MOUTH, FOR I HAVE HOPED IN YOUR ORDINANCES.

God's Word needs to be deep in our hearts before it can flow from our mouths. If we don't know the ordinances of the Lord, we won't know how to answer questions about the truth. We want God's Word to infiltrate the core of who we are. When we are consistently craving the Scriptures, we are prepared for anything this life throws at us. May the Word never be taken out of our minds, hearts and lives.

I love when I'm talking with someone about the Lord and I state a Bible verse I didn't even know I knew! It makes me realize that God's Word has been ingrained in my heart. I have God's Word in my heart to guard me against temptation and to testify of the truth. When you hope in God's ordinances you are embracing a hope that is 100 percent sure. Hoping in the Lord means hoping in facts that come from the Father, and no one can take away those eternal truths. May God's Word infiltrate your heart and fill your mind. Be so full of truth that you can't help but to share the good news.

44 SO SHALL I KEEP YOUR LAW CONTINUALLY, FOREVER AND EVER.

The psalmist wanted to keep God's Word continually. What an honorable and noble desire. We can keep God's Word through His strength and with the Holy Spirit's help. To be a consistent Christian, we need to be continually in His law, allowing it to change our hearts. If God's Word is not affecting our hearts, it will have no eternal impact on our lives. God's Word will always exist; it is the only thing we can take to heaven.

I fell in love with Jesus when I began reading the Bible years ago. I realized that the words in the Bible weren't just historical words, they were transformative words. I love the Scriptures so much because God uses them to define who I am, why I am here and what I'm called to do. They have changed my heart, my desires and life.

While you are on this earth, soak in the Scriptures on a continual basis so that you may grow, flourish and thrive in your faith. It's a privilege to daily dig into God's decrees. Personalize God's precepts as He uses them to speak directly to your heart and your life situation. Enjoy every minute of it.

45 AND I WILL WALK AT LIBERTY, FOR I SEEK YOUR PRECEPTS.

The psalmist is saying that obedience to God's Word brings a life of freedom. We get to know His ways by daily delving into His precepts. Submission to His precepts sets us free from bondage. It is futile to live for ourselves and rely upon our own wisdom. The more we seek God and are obedient to Him, the more we walk in wisdom and the freer we become. Reading the whole counsel of God puts life into perspective, making clear to us the priorities of life.

Bondage comes when we abandon God's ways. There's no freedom like the freedom I get from walking in the Lord's ways. When I seek the Lord through His Word, He lavishes on me peace and joy far above what this world offers. I absolutely love seeking the Lord through the Scriptures. Read the Word of God and simply do what it says with the wisdom that God gives. He wants you to live in the true freedom that He offers.

46 I WILL SPEAK OF YOUR TESTIMONIES ALSO BEFORE KINGS, AND WILL NOT BE ASHAMED.

Realizing the freedom in living out God's Word, the psalmist is able to live a life of boldness. When we base our lives upon the Word of the Lord, no person of stature will bring inhibition to our hearts. No person of status will hinder us from speaking up. The truth emboldens our lives to such an extent that we don't mind any negative pushback for what we believe. It's worth it.

Speak the testimonies before any person who inquires of you. Use your voice to be a truth teller in this tainted world we live in. Stand on the rock of God's truth and speak of the ways that God has worked in your life. There is absolutely no need to be ashamed of the words that God has given to His children. They are words that are solid and sure; words that have changed lives and hearts.

I believe that life is too short to be ashamed of living boldly for my faith. I have nothing to be ashamed about. I don't want to look back at my life and realize I did not have eternal impact for the Lord in this life. I want to look back and know that I boldly lived my life not for myself but for the Lord. You can be so bold when you speak with complete surety knowing that every word of God is true. Believe God's Word with all your heart, take it in, and give it out.

47 AND I WILL DELIGHT MYSELF IN YOUR COMMANDMENTS, WHICH I LOVE.

The psalmist makes it clear that delighting in God's Word is a choice. As believers we don't have to wait for certain feelings to come to us to delight in the Lord's words. The Bible is something to fall in love with and look forward to reading every day. I can relate to the psalmist's love for God's commandments. Of course for the psalmist he didn't have the whole Word of God like we do today. So what a joy we have to dig into the whole counsel of God!

I am thoroughly blessed that I get to read the Bible freely anytime I want. To be able to dig into a book, a chapter or a verse is something I sometimes take for granted. I am thankful that I have the Bible as a blueprint for everyday life. The more I read the Bible, the more I delight in it and fall in love with it. You will have such joy as a result of getting to know and implementing God's ways in your everyday life. Fall in love with His Word and delight in His ways. Get deep in the decrees that God has given you to meditate and ponder.

48 MY HANDS ALSO I WILL LIFT UP TO YOUR COMMANDMENTS, WHICH I LOVE, AND I WILL MEDITATE ON YOUR STATUTES.

We don't worship God's Word, but we do worship the God who breathed it into existence. He used His people to get His Word out to a broken and lost world. Hold the Scriptures up as the very words of God and let those words shape and mold you into who He wants you to be. Allow yourself to be accountable to God's statutes as you meditate and ponder what they say.

When I meditate upon the Scripture, I truly see God moving in my life as He clearly guides my every step. As I ponder what God says, He confirms things that He has already been speaking to me. God's Word percolates in my mind throughout the day and my countenance is lifted and my heart rejoices.

Let your heart be corrected and affected by God's amazing Word. Fall in love with it. The way to live is contained in Scripture; every time you read it your very life is shaped by it. You are blessed to have the whole counsel of God. Don't take His Word for granted but give in to what it says and allow the Lord to refine your mind and life.

49 REMEMBER THE WORD TO YOUR SERVANT, UPON WHICH YOU HAVE CAUSED ME TO HOPE.

When God gives us a promise, we have the opportunity to turn His promises into prayers. The psalmist hopes in God's promises to him. Praying before, during, and after we read God's Word is a good action to take as it causes us to hope. *Hope* in the Bible does not disappoint or let us down. *Hope* is a sure thing.

When God gives me a promise, I don't put a time limit on that promise. Instead, I pray for patience while I hide that promise in my heart until God gives me the green light. Although some have taken years to come to pass, I've realized over and over that God wants me to pray through His promises. Often God prepares me so that by the time He says go, I'm equipped for the next step.

If God has given you a promise, pray about it on a consistent basis. Every time He gives you a promise, that promise is in the process of coming to pass. God's promises will cause you to hope and pray for His timing and perfect plan. So keep praying until those promises come to pass according to His will.

50 THIS IS MY COMFORT IN MY AFFLICTION, FOR YOUR WORD HAS GIVEN ME LIFE.

The psalmist reflects upon the fact that the Word of God has given him life. He writes of a certain affliction and how the Scriptures bring him comfort. The way to know about eternal life, salvation, and all things spiritual is from the Word of God. What a blessing to know that the Word brings life and comfort in our chaotic circumstances.

Before I was saved and began reading the Bible, I had no firm foundation to build my life upon. My life was built on sand and it was constantly struck down by storms. It wasn't until I constructed my life on Christ that I could see clearly through the storms. God wants to reassure you with His Word and establish you in the faith. Continue to find comfort in the Scriptures whether you are on the mountaintop praising Him or in the storm crying out to Him. He's holding you close and wants to remind you that He is the way to life and the conduit that brings total comfort. May you always have God's Word on your heart and mind so that when storms come, you can stay founded upon the rock.

51 THE PROUD HAVE ME IN GREAT DERISION, YET I DO NOT TURN ASIDE FROM YOUR LAW.

There will always be those who are proud, who ridicule us for holding fast to God's Word. They think we are wasting our time on something that doesn't exist or matter. Pray for them. The Lord doesn't want them to perish. Stick to the Scriptures in spite of derision and verbal attacks. Let no one and nothing stop you from seeking God through His Word. Love your enemies and pray for those who push the truth away. Oftentimes your mockers are stuck in the miry clay of the world and they are helpless and hopeless.

Before I came to the Lord, I was a mocker. I didn't know the gospel and I didn't care to hear about it. Yet I had friends who cared enough for my soul to share the Word with me despite my mockery of them. Then one day, what they said struck me and worked in my heart. I went from being a hater to being heaven bound.

Just like the Lord saved you, God wants to save those who are angry toward Him. Stand strong in the Scriptures and let nothing deter you from speaking His decrees. You have strength from God to face any pushback from people who are against the Lord. Pray for those people, share the Word with them, and love them with God's love.

52 I REMEMBERED YOUR JUDGMENTS OF OLD, O LORD, AND HAVE COMFORTED MYSELF.

The psalmist may have had his confidence crushed, according to verse 51, from those who had derision toward him for following God's Word. But as he remembers God's judgments, he was able to gain comfort from his Creator.

Diving daily into Scripture brings such comfort to our hearts no matter what situation we are facing. I can't tell you how many times I've been in turmoil, only to open God's Word and my attitude and outlook completely turn around. In my life God has used His Word to change my chaos into calm, my anxiety into peace, and my difficulties into deliverance.

How many times have you dug into Scripture and had the Lord speak directly to your heart giving you abundant peace? God's Word, when read and applied, will change your heart from unsettled to serene. Even a good night's sleep in the most comfortable bed cannot compare to the heart rest that the Word brings. Delve into the Scriptures and you will fall completely in love with God's words to your heart and situation. Remember what He has said and let His truth sink into your soul bringing you peace and heart rest.

53 INDIGNATION HAS TAKEN HOLD OF ME BECAUSE OF THE WICKED, WHO FORSAKE YOUR LAW.

The psalmist clearly recognized his enemies' great sin, forsaking God's Word. They may have heard the Scriptures from the people of God, but they had no desire to get to know what God said. They were most likely the same men who mocked the psalmist because he believed his Maker wrote the words that he held onto. The wicked suppress the truth and pretend it doesn't exist. The wicked laugh at the idea of God using His children to pen the precepts that still exist today. The Bible is the best-selling book of all time and the most stolen book in the world. God's Word existed back in those days and it's still going strong today. The wicked can mock all they want, but no one and nothing can stop the spread of the truth from those who know it and enact it.

When I share God's Word, I feel like I come alive. As I share verses, a fire ignites in my heart and passion erupts in my soul. I realize time and time again that people need the hope and help that is in God's Word. Use God's Word today to speak to your own heart and to flow forth to all who would listen. We can make an impact by imparting the Scriptures to those around us.

54 YOUR STATUTES HAVE BEEN MY SONGS IN THE HOUSE OF MY PILGRIMAGE.

As we read God's Word it stirs in us praise for what He says. The statutes of the Lord are so incredibly encouraging and exhortative that we can't help but worship Him as a result. As we pass through this world, we are pilgrims, not permanent residents. The one thing that we can hold onto as sojourners on this earth is the Word of the Lord. We base our lives upon it! May we not only scratch the surface, let's passionately soak in the Scriptures and let them affect every corner of our hearts.

Often I've been so overwhelmed by the Scriptures that I couldn't help but respond in worship. There have been times where the Lord has spoken so clearly to me that I would just stop and thank Him in prayer. When I remember that the point of my life is not to lay a foundation here but to forge ahead in the faith, I can't help but praise the Lord.

When you routinely get into God's Word, you'll want to worship the Lord as you are going about your day-to-day routine. The Lord can use His Word to break up your self-motivated routine and cause you to give in to His supernatural leading. Your questions will be answered as you allow the Word to work in your heart. May the truth from the Lord cause an adoration toward Him that pours out of your life and influences others.

55 I REMEMBER YOUR NAME IN THE NIGHT, O LORD, AND I KEEP YOUR LAW.

At night, after we've had a long day, we're drained and we don't want to exert any more energy, we just want to shut off our minds and tune out. But we have to remember that at nighttime is when we are susceptible to sin; it is when we need to keep God's Word the most. You see, in our weakness we can quickly become apathetic and give in to sin. We have to use God's Word as a guard during those times where we know we are the weakest. Many people are the weakest at the end of the day when their guard is down.

Over the years I've learned what times and surroundings that I get tempted the most. Now that I know when and where I'm the weakest, I can avoid those places and scenarios so I don't give in to sin. Know when you are the weakest and plan to put processes in place to stay in God's precepts. Be on guard by being in God's Word during your weakest moments. At the end of the day you'll want to be on guard so as not to give in to fleshly desires. Stay seeking Him all the way up until you head hits the pillow at night.

56 THIS HAS BECOME MINE, BECAUSE I KEPT YOUR PRECEPTS.

The psalmist is triumphant because of God's Word. Good comes from getting into the Bible and doing what it says. As we faithfully live according to the Word of the Lord, we can have victory in every single aspect of our lives. As believers we realize that God is keeping us, and we are blessed.

One guy asked me once how I can stay pure. I replied to him that it is impossible to stay pure without God's Word, God's strength and God's leading. I could not live an undefiled life without being dependent upon and delivered by the Lord. The Book that we believe in keeps us from sin and sanctifies our very lives.

Don't compartmentalize God's Word but let it pierce every part of who you are. Know that you are triumphant when you let God's Word into all areas of your life. The Bible is a personal love letter teaching you how to live and reminding you of God's heart toward you. He loves you and wants the best for your life. And the best for your life is to live out your calling as it becomes clear through prayer and His Word.

57 YOU ARE MY PORTION, O LORD; I HAVE SAID THAT I WOULD KEEP YOUR WORDS.

These are the words of a believer who finds complete satisfaction in God. The Lord is our portion; He brings replenishment to our weary souls. Because the Lord is our portion, it's not a burden to keep His Word. It is a joy and blessing to follow the One who knows where He is going and what He is doing. When we see God as having the ultimate authority, the result on our part will be beautiful obedience.

God fills every void that I have as He is our nourishment and supplier of truth. As I seek the Lord, I realize that the spiritual nutrients I desperately need are found in the pages of Scripture. Delving into God's decrees is overwhelmingly beneficial to my heart—His Word is my plated food that I get to partake in every day. Make sure that the Lord is your portion day in and day out. Feed off of His faithfulness. Find nourishment in His Word and the result will be a satisfied soul and solid strength.

58 I ENTREATED YOUR FAVOR WITH MY WHOLE HEART; BE MERCIFUL TO ME ACCORDING TO YOUR WORD.

In this verse the psalmist speaks about the Lord's favor. This term *Your favor* actually translates to "Your face." The writer makes it clear that he sought the Lord's face—but not only did he seek God's face, he sought the Lord's face *with his whole heart*. The idea is that he had a sense of urgency in seeking God. Not only did he have a sense of urgency, he also recognized his inability apart from God, as reflected in the phrase, "Be merciful to me." Mercy is not getting what we deserve. The Lord Jesus is why we have mercy; He extends His mercy to sinful humanity. How amazing that the Lord would extend all spiritual riches to His undeserving children.

When I truly meditate upon God's mercy in my own life, I am blown away. I cannot believe that I'm still alive and that God has kept me through the times where I made the worst decisions. God's mercy is marvelous, and I never want to forget His mercy toward me. Not only do I marvel at God's mercy, I want to live this short life for Him in all that I do. I don't want to forget that I only have so much time for this life on this earth, so I need to live it wisely.

Seek the Lord with a sense of urgency and ask Him what He'd have you to do. Let Him lead every facet of your life to make an eternal impact. He has favor upon you and He wants to use you greatly. Stay in His Word so His will becomes clear for your life, then you can enact it for eternity.

59 I THOUGHT ABOUT MY WAYS, AND TURNED MY FEET TO YOUR TESTIMONIES.

As the psalmist was in God's Word, it caused him to reflect on his own life and the way it was going. Our ways may seem right but apart from the Lord's Word, we will head in the wrong direction and end up at the wrong destination. When we turn our feet toward the Lord's testimonies, then we will be on the right track.

Thinking back to my ways before I met the Lord, sometimes I shudder at where I went and what I did.

I was making my own way in this world and it was leading to dead end after dead end. Yet, that reflection causes me to appreciate and be elated about how I am now walking with the Lord and living according to His Word. When I remember my time of ungodly living, I realize how lost I was, and I contemplate how good God is for rescuing me.

You have the blessing of turning your feet toward the Lord's testimonies and walking in His ways. You were not made to live life for self, you were made to live your life for the Lord. Abandon your self-led life now; it's time to let God lead as you continue on His trail every step of the way.

60 I MADE HASTE, AND DID NOT DELAY TO KEEP YOUR COMMANDMENTS.

This verse indicates a sure sign of revival. When we make haste, we move quickly toward something. Since we don't live any longer for ourselves, we press forward with a sense of urgency for the kingdom of God. We understand that time is short and the time to live fully for the Lord is now! There is no time to waste. When we make haste, we have to make sure that our focal point is the Lord, nothing and no one else. If we are in a hurry but going the wrong way, we will end up crashing. But if we are heading toward the Lord in haste and we hang onto Him, our hearts will be alive and on fire for the things of God.

I don't want to waste my life walking on a road that is not purposely paved for me. I have no desire to wander off of the path God has for me. He knows what's best for my life. He knows which way I need to go, and so I want to travel on that trail full steam ahead. Don't delay living fully for the Lord. He wants to use you mightily in this life. All you have to do is make sure He is the center of your affections and your motivation for every action you take. Stay on the path God has for you and remember that you are just along for the ride. What an amazing ride it is!

61 THE CORDS OF THE WICKED HAVE BOUND ME, BUT I HAVE NOT FORGOTTEN YOUR LAW.

The psalmist had enemies who were fighting against him, causing adversity in his life and most likely bringing discouragement to his mind. Yet, he had not forgotten the Lord's law.

How many times have we faced hardship and the Lord brings Bible verses to our minds? How many times have people discouraged us, and the Holy Spirit speaks encouragement to our hearts? How many times have we been down, and the Lord reminds us to look up? The Lord transfers Scripture from our hearts to our heads so we can face any adversity and get through any trial.

God extracts the Word from my heart during those moments when I need Him the most. The more I soak in the Scriptures, the more truth I have to draw from in the midst of troublesome times. Remember God's Word when the world gets you down. Recite Scripture when your countenance falls. Pray that God would bring His Word to your remembrance resulting in perfect peace and radical rest.

FALLING IN LOVE WITH GOD'S WORD

62 AT MIDNIGHT I WILL RISE TO GIVE THANKS TO YOU, BECAUSE OF YOUR RIGHTEOUS JUDGMENTS.

The Word of God is so ingrained in the heart of the psalmist that he actually wakes up to thank God for His Word. The psalmist sincerely thanks God, rising at midnight when no one else is around. He gains refreshment from the Scriptures rather than from the world (which is impossible). The fact that he rose up at night shows his reverence toward the Lord. The psalmist sacrifices sleep to seek the Lord.

When the Word of God is permeating my mind and running through my veins, I cease to fear whatever may come before me. When I ingest God's Word it leads to refinement in my life and refreshment for my soul.

No time is ever the wrong time to seek God through His Word. Thank the Lord today for He has given you His precious precepts. You have before you God's perfect Word, the most powerful Book in existence. Read the Bible, dig into it, and let it speak to your heart and refresh your soul. And whether we purposely wake up or our sleep is interrupted, may we take the time to thank and praise God.

63 I AM A COMPANION OF ALL WHO FEAR YOU, AND OF THOSE WHO KEEP YOUR PRECEPTS.

The psalmist expresses his gratitude for those who share his passion for the Lord's precepts. How wonderful it is to have fellowship with like-minded believers who hold the Word of God up as the standard for spiritual living. Not springboard teaching but straight

Scripture. Sharing with each other about how impacting the Word is to our personal lives truly makes for genuine fellowship and connection.

I cannot and will not disconnect the Word of God from my everyday life. I will not compartmentalize the Scripture or only use it when I'm in trouble. I base my life upon what the Bible says because it is the undefiled Word of God. You have the great privilege to daily dig into the words that the Lord wrote through His disciples. These divine words have the power to work in your heart and lead your life. When you're in the midst of difficult times, seek God through His Word so that you can hear His voice and follow His lead. May we honestly talk to one another about how the Lord is using His Word to speak to our very life situation. As believers may we fall in love with the Bible and base our lives upon it.

64 THE EARTH, O LORD, IS FULL OF YOUR MERCY; TEACH ME YOUR STATUTES.

God's mercy is absolutely marvelous. We can receive His new mercies every single day. The psalmist felt the goodness of God filling the earth and the mercies of God expanding across the universe. When we realize the awesome greatness of God, we will praise Him and seek Him. As we respond to the Lord in this way, we come to a spiritual awareness that incites a reverence for God.

I am overwhelmed by the Lord's perfect love toward us, His imperfect people. May you daily pray that the Lord will teach you His Word. There is always more to learn. According to your situation God can use one single verse to speak several different ways. Revel in God's Word today!

65 YOU HAVE DEALT WELL WITH YOUR SERVANT, O LORD, ACCORDING TO YOUR WORD.

Think about all the amazing ways that the Lord has dealt with us. Not only has He chosen us, He blesses us, leads us, grants us grace and mercy—God is so good.

The Bible is the blueprint for our lives. We should not make up our own guidelines for living because God has already prepared our way. The Word of God is the litmus test for how we are to live, what we're to do, where we go and why. We don't heed man's word about life, we heed God's Word. "His divine power has given to us all things that pertain to life and godliness, through the knowledge of Him who called us by glory and virtue" (2 Peter 1:3).

When I ponder the way that God has dealt with me, I'm overwhelmed with joy and gratification. He has called me, led me and blessed me. God deals lovingly with you as well; with such grace and so much mercy. Don't take it for granted but marvel in His lovingkindness toward your life.

66 TEACH ME GOOD JUDGMENT AND KNOWLEDGE, FOR I BELIEVE YOUR COMMANDMENTS.

The psalmist asks the Lord to teach him right judgment and godly knowledge. He understands that the Lord's way as laid out in His Word is the right way. When we truly believe that Scripture is the guidebook for practical Christian living, we will live in complete submission. In other words, when we fully believe that God's Word emanates from God Himself, we will stand firm and hold fast to the Scriptures and fall in love with what He says. As the Holy Spirit speaks to you, cling to His commandments with your whole heart and receive His conviction.

Everything that the Lord has said to me through His Word is good and has led me to hold onto God even more. I have total faith in the Bible. I have no doubt that it is written from God for His children. You were made to live the life that the Lord has laid out in His Word. Ask Him to teach you the truth on a daily basis and you'll spiritually grow exponentially. Let His commandments cover you and seek His strength to live them out.

67 BEFORE I WAS AFFLICTED I WENT ASTRAY, BUT NOW I KEEP YOUR WORD.

In those moments where we have been led astray, the Lord brings His Word to our minds to guide us back. Conviction leads to correction and the result is getting right with the Lord. Affliction has an effect that can either lure us away from God or draw us closer to Him. When God's Word has been ingrained in our hearts, the truth will prevail in what we do and say.

Soon after I became a believer I drifted away from the Lord. I was so lost and ashamed, I didn't think God could ever forgive me or take me back. Yet, I came back to Him and He welcomed me, restarted me and refined my life greatly.

When we lose our way, the Lord patiently waits for us to heed His Word, repent and return to Him. Just like the prodigal son, we can return to the Father and He will not be angry with us; instead, He will rejoice that we came home. God's heart is to save the lost and welcome back those who have gone astray. Let God's Word lead your life. Through those times when you are tempted, the Scriptures will keep you grounded. Stay established in God's Word and allow His strength to carry you in your weakness.

68 YOU ARE GOOD, AND DO GOOD; TEACH ME YOUR STATUTES.

The psalmist did not get super bitter toward God when going through hardships. He recognized that trials did not mean that God's nature changed. God remains good when things in life do not line up with how we think they should go. No matter what the situation and through the most intense storms, we can depend on God being consistently good—all the time.

Admittedly there have been times when I was going through intense trials that I questioned God's goodness. I wondered what in the world He was doing. Yet, looking back I realized that every time He was using my trials to work in radical ways in my life. He was using my rough circumstances, as well as my blessed situations, for the good (Romans 8:28).

Your vision can become clouded as you go through rough circumstances but remember that God's nature stays the same. He is good all the time and He'll get you through every difficult season. As the Lord does good things in your life, pray that His Word gets ingrained in your heart so you'll remember His goodness. Your view of God will be correct as you constantly dig into His statutes.

69 THE PROUD HAVE FORGED A LIE AGAINST ME, BUT I WILL KEEP YOUR PRECEPTS WITH MY WHOLE HEART.

Those who are prideful usually hate the humble and kind person. With pride welled up in their hearts, they are often self-focused and resentful of those who do the right things with the right attitude. The psalmist had a humility about him and therefore, was hated by his enemies. But the psalmist did not let the proud who were against him alter his seeking after the Scriptures. He continued to keep God's precepts with his whole heart.

I find that the more I stay in God's Word on a consistent basis, the more my heart is honed in to God's heart. I so believe in the reading of God's Word on a consistent basis because it is the catalyst to spiritual growth. My character is shaped by the life-changing Word of God. My behavior is a result of the character that God builds in me as I read His Word.

As you really get into the decrees of the Lord, you'll be able to retain a godly character even when opposition occurs. You'll be able to live for the Lord even if lies are forged against you. Stick to God's Word and draw strength from the promises He gives you. Let the Bible shape your character into the person He has called you to be.

70 THEIR HEART IS AS FAT AS GREASE, BUT I DELIGHT IN YOUR LAW.

The expression *heart as fat as grease* means "a heart that's dull of hearing, insensitive and indulging in excess," and here refers to the spiritual heart. The heart is the core of who we are as human beings. When we are driven by things of the world, then we can be led astray and fall in love with things that leave our hearts empty. But when we delight in the law of the Lord, we are filled and focused on good and godly things.

I had wasted so much time focusing on things that make no difference in this world. I delighted in activities and actions that did not bring me to a place of joy and fulfillment. When I came to delight in God's Word, I grew deeper in love with Him and my heart became more grounded in the things of the Lord. You have a choice to delight in the law of the Lord or delight in the lust of the flesh. One leads to life and one leads to death. Whichever you choose, you'll be dedicated to what you delight in. May you choose to focus on God's Word, rather than this dark world.

71 IT IS GOOD FOR ME THAT I HAVE BEEN AFFLICTED, THAT I MAY LEARN YOUR STATUTES.

God's Word becomes more transparent when we are in the fire of affliction. We never pray to face trials but when trials come, we can cling to the beautiful promises of the Lord. Often we don't learn much when things are going well. Usually success doesn't teach humility or dependency. But when we are facing hardship and affliction, the Scriptures become more real to us. The things of this world dims and the truth of God lights up. So as we go through affliction, it produces a clarity of God's promises to our hearts and lives.

When I'm in a raging storm the Word of God illuminates my path. Don't fret as you go through frustrating times but hold fast to the Word. Difficulties are good because they drive us to the Scriptures for answers and God meets us in the midst of every rough moment. You may be facing some trials right now. Instead of despising the trials, stay dependent upon the Lord and know that He will meet you where you're at.

72 THE LAW OF YOUR MOUTH IS BETTER TO ME THAN THOUSANDS OF COINS OF GOLD AND SILVER.

Riches have been the focus of many people throughout the centuries. People have made their goal to attain wealth in order to be set for life and be happy forever. Yet, even those who have achieved their monetary goals and financial successes are left feeling empty. They are not satisfied with the money that they have finally accumulated. The psalmist is entirely correct in his contrast between riches and the Word. Oftentimes riches do not give wisdom but they excuse wisdom and cause complete foolishness. The consumption of money has left many blind to the important matters of life.

When money was my focus, I never attained any sort of happiness or fulfillment. Money had never given me peace or permanent security. The Lord is my peace and rest—not money or material items. God's Word leads to real wisdom, riches and a fullness that no amount of money can bring. You are blessed to be able to draw your riches from the well of God's Word. Do not let money reign and rule in your life. Instead, allow the Lord to consume you and His Word to satisfy your soul.

73 YOUR HANDS HAVE MADE ME AND FASHIONED ME; GIVE ME UNDERSTANDING, THAT I MAY LEARN YOUR COMMANDMENTS.

It is clear to the psalmist that God is the Creator of the world. How great that the Lord has created the universe and still thinks about us. He cares about what we face and struggle with in this life. Viewing the Lord as our Creator will give us a reverence for His Word and His ways. He fashioned us and formed us out of love. Now we have the privilege to follow Him and live out His calling for us. What a blessing to know that our magnificent Creator cares deeply for us and has an amazing future for us to fulfill.

Sometimes I feel like no one really cares about what I go through or face in this life. It's in those times that I'm reminded that God cares about the trials I face and the temptations that try and take me down. The Lord sees me and He is with me every step of my life. He created me and sustains me out of grace. You are the Lord's workmanship—He created you, He keeps you, and He loves you so much. What you go through matters to God and He is right there with you every step of the way.

74 THOSE WHO FEAR YOU WILL BE GLAD WHEN THEY SEE ME, BECAUSE I HAVE HOPED IN YOUR WORD.

The psalmist was a good witness for the Lord because he hoped in the Scriptures. As our lives line up with the Word of God and people see the sure hope that we have, we're drawing them to live for Him. When we are constantly in God's Word, following His ways and His will, it causes those who see us to stand in awe of who He is.

I think about the Lord and stand in awe of what He has done in my heart and life. I'm so incredibly blessed and humbled by His work. How immeasurably good He is!

Gladness is a result of running your race of faith in this life. When you hope in God's Word, you believe that He has a future for you. Let Him lead every season of your life and be glad knowing you are in His will. It truly brings joy to the heart of those who follow His calling. And let those who see you be glad because you hope in His Word.

75 I KNOW, O LORD, THAT YOUR JUDGMENTS ARE RIGHT, AND THAT IN FAITHFULNESS YOU HAVE AFFLICTED ME.

The psalmist knows that God's judgments are righteous. God is faithful and His judgments are 100 percent accurate 100 percent of the time. Even when God corrects us, He is just. The Lord's correction stems from His perfect love. His discipline is to ensure we are on the road of His will.

When God corrects me through His Word, it allows me to see clearly what I need to work on and where

I am weak so I can adjust my priorities and realign my life with Him. Allow God's faithful love for you to penetrate your heart and every area of your life. Believe that His judgments are for the benefit of building in you a passion for heavenly things, not earthly treasures. God is faithful to get you back on track.

You are loved and lovingly corrected by the One you want to live for. When you surrender completely to the Lord's correction and let Him fight your battles, you will soon have victory over your afflictions.

76 LET, I PRAY, YOUR MERCIFUL KINDNESS BE FOR MY COMFORT, ACCORDING TO YOUR WORD TO YOUR SERVANT.

So often we forget about the Lord's mercies and we condemn ourselves for past actions. Yes, we are faulty and we have failed, but the Lord is faithful to shower us with mercy every single day. We don't get the judgment we deserve. The Lord withholds His judgment on us because His mercy is abundant toward His children. When I think of how God has not given me what I truly deserve, I am in awe and overwhelmed. It's almost unbelievable how good God is. But then I seek Him through His Word and I'm reminded over and over that God really is that good all the time, every day.

Be comforted with the Lord's mercy and let His kindness fill your soul. As you serve the Lord, you can walk in relief knowing that the Lord's mercy is never ending. And because God has mercy on you, remember to have mercy on yourself. Don't condemn yourself for what God has forgiven you for. Be free knowing that the Lord's kindness and mercies are there for the receiving.

77 LET YOUR TENDER MERCIES COME TO ME, THAT I MAY LIVE; FOR YOUR LAW IS MY DELIGHT.

As he dug into God's Word, the psalmist understood God's tender mercies. As we inquire into the Lord's decrees, we realize we are alive and able to thrive because of God's amazing mercies. Our hearts are filled with joy as we daily dive into the Scriptures. The Lord's powerful love toward us should cause us to walk in His countenance.

God's love has held me through the most intense hardships. Before I was a believer, I didn't know what true love was. When I began walking with the Lord, seeking Him, His love radically changed my life and consumed my heart.

When you mess up, His mercy is there for the taking. God loves you and wants you to know that His mercies are new every single morning of every single day. Marvel at God's mercy and know that He absolutely loves you. As you read God's Word, you'll realize the truth of His grace and mercy, causing you to fall in love with Him even more.

78 LET THE PROUD BE ASHAMED, FOR THEY TREATED ME WRONGFULLY WITH FALSEHOOD; BUT I WILL MEDITATE ON YOUR PRECEPTS.

There are times when people come against us and fail us. People will let us down, break their promise, or speak lies against us. The psalmist said they should be ashamed. The good news is that God's Word is truth. In a world full of lies, we can meditate upon the Scriptures and know truth will always stand.

In the past some people have come against me and used me for their selfish gain. There have been gossipers and backstabbers who attempted to tear down what God has built up. My response was to gain wisdom from God's Word on how to deal with the situation.

Living in a fallen, broken, sin-filled world you have been wronged by people, and it hurt you. But as you meditate on the Lord's Word, you'll be assured, comforted, cleansed, and lifted. You'll be filled with "hope that doesn't disappoint" (Romans 5:5). Keep your eyes upon Him and His precepts; He will restore you and completely heal your heart.

79 LET THOSE WHO FEAR YOU TURN TO ME, THOSE WHO KNOW YOUR TESTIMONIES.

The psalmist believed that not all his enemies would reject God completely. We cannot count people out when it comes to the kingdom of God. There are those who fear God and know His testimonies, but they are lukewarm in their spiritual walk. We have the privilege of shining as lights to complacent believers. As Christians we get to sharpen one another in the faith. May we encourage and exhort each other to stay on the track that God has laid out for us.

I've come to realize that as long as someone has breath in their lungs, there is hope that they would accept Jesus. I do not want to give up on people who are blind to the truth or are backslidden because they could still turn around and get saved or return to the Lord. I would rather pray for them and use every God-given opportunity to share the hope that is found in Jesus. Be a light to unbelievers, love your enemies, and encourage those who are struggling. If you know a weak believer who needs encouragement, be that person who prays for them, who has fellowship with them and lifts up their countenance with the testimonies of the Lord.

80 LET MY HEART BE BLAMELESS REGARDING YOUR STATUTES, THAT I MAY NOT BE ASHAMED.

As the psalmist closely connected with the Lord, he sought to be blameless. To be blameless doesn't mean to be perfect, it means living a life that is cohesive to the perfect One. Being blameless means one establishes his life upon the Lord and seeks God's strength to adhere to the Scriptures. When we follow the perfect Word of God, we will never be ashamed.

If we live according to the world we will be unhinged and lost. As we walk according to God's Word we have nothing to be ashamed of. We are secure in the Savior as His Word assures us that we are on the right track. We never have to be ashamed believing and adhering to the truth.

"The mouth of the righteous speaks wisdom, and his tongue talks of justice. The law of his God is in his heart; none of his steps shall slide" (Psalm 37:30-31). Seek Him through prayer and the Scriptures and you'll gain strength to live a life that glorifies God. As you live your life according to biblical principles, your heart will be blameless, pleasing the Father.

81 MY SOUL FAINTS FOR YOUR SALVATION, BUT I HOPE IN YOUR WORD.

Weary and tired, the psalmist was at his end. We've all been there—we're so extremely busy we're worn out and left with no strength! Yet, even in those moments and seasons of life we can cling to the Word in pure hope. When the Bible speaks of *hope*, it is a "hope that does not disappoint" (Romans 5:5). God's Word is sure and His promises always come to pass.

I've learned that the only hope that doesn't let me down is the hope I have in the Lord. He is my hope and my sure foundation. Even when I'm at my end and I feel like I can't go on, I rest upon God's promises. You may feel weak and tired, you may be worn out by life and it may seem like you have nothing left. Keep hoping in God's Word and let the Lord speak to you through the Scriptures and regain your strength from Him to forge ahead in the faith.

When things are difficult, it brings us such comfort and joy to look to the future when we'll be with the Lord in heaven. For our hope is in Christ and our future is eternity with our God.

82 MY EYES FAIL FROM SEARCHING YOUR WORD, SAYING, "WHEN WILL YOU COMFORT ME?"

The psalmist studied the Scriptures to such an extent that his eyes were strained and blurry. What a testimony and testament to being faithful to read God's Word. The Scriptures are full of promises that are truly a treasure trove to all who search them. The more we get into God's Word, the richer our spiritual life will become.

Just as the psalmist searched so diligently and received comfort from the Creator of the universe, so shall we gain comfort and clarity during times of conflict. God works powerfully through His precepts.

Many times in my life I've had tough and unsettling times. I open the Bible and immediately the verses speak clearly to my heart. God works powerfully to hold my heart together when I feel scattered. He reminds me that He loves me when I feel empty and alone. As you make time to meditate upon God's Word, He will speak into your situation. His love will engulf you and His peace will wash over you.

83 FOR I HAVE BECOME LIKE A WINESKIN IN SMOKE, YET I DO NOT FORGET YOUR STATUTES.

The psalmist felt weak and brittle, like an old wineskin that has turned dry and black with smoke. He felt dry spiritually.

When our hearts are dry in the desert, we need the water of the Word to wash over us. I've had my share of dry times where I was just going through the motions. Yet, even in those seasons I knew the only way to stay hydrated was by heeding the Lord through reading His Word.

In those moments where you feel extremely dry and weak spiritually, don't forget His statutes. Cling to God's Word until the Lord speaks. His Word will be like an oasis in the midst of barren land. "Whoever desires, let him take the water of life freely" (Revelation 22:17).

84 HOW MANY ARE THE DAYS OF YOUR SERVANT? WHEN WILL YOU EXECUTE JUDGMENT ON THOSE WHO PERSECUTE ME?

This is one of the few verses in Psalm 119 that does not actually mention God's Word. The psalmist was feeling weak as his enemies were coming against him, so he cried out to God for help. Seeking the Lord in desperation is actually a trait ingrained in the people of God. As we live our lives completely sold out for the Lord, there will be those people who will constantly come against us.

Years ago while on a job, I'll never forget, a co-worker had picked an argument with me. I knew he was trying to provoke me because I was a Christian. He kept going and going until I got heated. A fellow employee, who was also a Christian, nudged me to settle down, saying it's not worth the argument. So I had to pray and repent for being angry.

The fact is that sometimes you'll feel infuriated by those who put pressure on you because you're living for the Lord. Still you can seek the Lord in His Word. Just as the psalmist, go to God and His precepts. "He will make your righteous reward shine like the dawn, your vindication like the noonday sun" (Psalm 37:6 NIV).

85 THE PROUD HAVE DUG PITS FOR ME, WHICH IS NOT ACCORDING TO YOUR LAW.

There are many people in this world who are against God. How they live and what they do are directly against the law of the Lord. The psalmist said that those who were against him were really against the Lord. The enemy is always trying to entrap us and destroy what God has built up in us. The devil will use people, places and situations to attempt to catch us when our guard is down. But the law of the Lord gives us discernment to know what a trap is and how to escape those traps.

The most confused and discouraging times in my life occurred when I had drifted away from God's Word, when I let the busyness of life lure me away from the ways of the Lord. But I soon came to realize that to be in fellowship with Him and to dig into His decrees was what I was created to do.

As you let the Scriptures seep into your heart and mind, continually ask Him for discernment so as not to get distracted. Keep your eyes upon God's precepts and the result will be a victorious freedom from those ungodly traps and carnal temptations. God's Word will keep you grounded, established and stable. "It is God who works in you both to will and to do for His good pleasure" (Philippians 2:13).

86 ALL YOUR COMMANDMENTS ARE FAITHFUL; THEY PERSECUTE ME WRONGFULLY; HELP ME!

In total contrast to the treachery of God's enemies, the psalmist found faithfulness in the Scriptures. Man's ways are corrupt and crafty, the works of the flesh. But God's Word is faithful; His promises are true. When we as believers are persecuted in various ways, we can openly and honestly cry out to the Lord for help.

There have been times where I struggled and wanted to give up. Yet the Lord met me in my weakness and filled me with His strength and the power to persevere. In those dark moments where it seems no one is with you, God is there. God is with you and He is for you. Dig into His decrees; they are an offensive weapon to fight the enemy, the world's ways and the flesh. Without the Lord, we will burn out and give up. "O my God, I trust in You; let me not be ashamed; let not my enemies triumph over me" (Psalm 25:2).

87 THEY ALMOST MADE AN END OF ME ON EARTH, BUT I DID NOT FORSAKE YOUR PRECEPTS.

The psalmist would not let anything cause him to forsake the Lord's precepts. When we throw the Bible on the bookshelf and never pick it up, we begin to forget the standards set by God. We are not striving to be perfect, but as we simply seek Him and grow in His Word, God is perfecting us. The more we consistently digest the decrees of God, the more we will be walking on the road of God's will and the more we will see the spiritual side of life clearly. If our Bibles are out of sight and out of mind, then our spiritual growth will cease and compromises in our Christian life will increase.

I've used God's Word as a weapon time and time again, especially during those times where my mind goes crazy—when I begin to get down and discouraged and my thoughts fill with major negativity. During those times I open the Scriptures and the Lord reminds me that "the thoughts He thinks toward me are thoughts of peace and not of evil" (Jeremiah 29:11). The Lord only fills me with His encouraging words and He lifts up my countenance like nothing else can.

You have the ammunition you need to fight against the spiritual hosts of wickedness that attempt to take you out. Use the Word of God to fend off thoughts that suppress your spiritual life. God's Word is a weapon you can use not only to protect you, but to propel you even further in the faith. Even when the enemy bombards you with doubts and attempts to lure you away from the Lord, do not forsake His Word.

88 REVIVE ME ACCORDING TO YOUR LOVINGKINDNESS, SO THAT I MAY KEEP THE TESTIMONY OF YOUR MOUTH.

Revive means "to give new life." The psalmist asks the Lord to revive him through the avenue of His lovingkindness. We couldn't do anything to revive our own hearts and our lives. All we could do is surrender to the Lord and He makes us new. God can transform our minds and hearts in an instant.

I've come to realize that every single one of us as believers influences someone. The words I speak and the actions I take reflect what's in my heart. Therefore, I want to make sure that my heart is filled with a fire to live for Jesus. We need a revival in this world, and it starts with our individual walks with the Lord.

You will make a great impact when you get into God's Word and live it out practically. The kingdom of God is built when the people of God wake up through revival. Seek God and ask Him to open your eyes fully to His will for your life—to ignite a fire of passion to live an abandoned life unto Him. Yield to God and stay focused on the Word. Be expectant for what God wants to do in your life.

89 FOREVER, O LORD, YOUR WORD IS SETTLED IN HEAVEN.

God's Word is unchanging. It is settled in heaven which means they will not change on earth. In other words, no one should add or take away from God's Word. The whole counsel of God is for the taking and not to be altered or misapplied. The Bible is the book that we base our lives upon. We can trust its veracity and we are to value the Word of God while on this earth.

Some would say that those who hold the Bible in high esteem are placing too much emphasis on the Bible. I would disagree—God has the first word and the final word; His Word lays out why we live and who we live for.

The more I read God's Word, the more I'm amazed. The way in which the Bible fits together perfectly astounds me and just grows my trust in the Lord that much more. We have the great privilege of living in a time where we have the whole counsel of God in our hands. We have the whole story, the complete Scriptures to dig into and draw from. What an amazing blessing that God's Word is unchanging and life-shaping. Enjoy it. Revel in it. Let it change your heart.

90 YOUR FAITHFULNESS ENDURES TO ALL GENERATIONS; YOU ESTABLISHED THE EARTH, AND IT ABIDES.

The Lord's faithfulness does not run out and will never run dry. As God's Word is settled in heaven, we see God's faithfulness through the ages. "In the beginning God created the heavens and the earth" (Genesis 1:1). The Lord masterfully established the earth with His words. If that doesn't amaze you, nothing will.

When I peer out at the ocean, mountains, the sunrises and sunsets, I can't help but think of the creative Artist who fashioned everything into existence. And for that reason, I stand in awe, and I want to daily take that amazement and relay it to my children and the next generation.

You have the opportunity to abide in Him in this generation as well. As you build the foundation of your life upon the Word of the Lord, you'll clearly see the faithfulness of God carry you from now into eternity.

91 THEY CONTINUE THIS DAY ACCORDING TO YOUR ORDINANCES, FOR ALL ARE YOUR SERVANTS.

From generation to generation people have clung to the Word of the Lord and lived according to God's ways. We can peer into the past and see how God has been faithful to His servants. It's a blessing to be a servant of the Lord and to follow His plan and purposes for us. When we heed God's decrees, we are living the way God designed us to live.

I have tried to live the way the world says I should live. The result was misery and emptiness. I acted like everything was okay, but nothing can satisfy a soul like the Savior of the world. Nothing can bring peace, rest and rejuvenation like the Lord. When I soak in the Scriptures regularly, I am so revived, built up and ready to continue on.

So make sure you are in God's Word on a continual basis. You are not called to be an occasional Christian; you are called to be a full-time Christian. It's not a compartmentalized faith system; it is a way of life. Allow the Word to continue to refine your life and correct your perspective. As Christians it's all about consistency—serving the Lord according to His ordinances.

92 UNLESS YOUR LAW HAD BEEN MY DELIGHT, I WOULD THEN HAVE PERISHED IN MY AFFLICTION.

Reading God's Word is not a drag or burdensome task, it is a blessing and a delight. When we open the Scriptures, we are preparing ourselves to hear the Lord speak to our personal situations. Something supernatural happens as the Lord uses the Scriptures to speak directly to what we are going through at that very moment. During his many afflictions the psalmist understood that the Lord sustained him.

Just like you, I've gone through major trials in my Christian life. Sometimes I forget that He is so incredibly faithful. Yet in hindsight, I can emphatically say that God has delivered me through every single difficulty. The Lord uses His Word not just to help us through small everyday trials, but His Word gives us strength through major afflictions.

Without the words from God you'd be lost, without hope and drifting in this dark world. The Lord knows exactly what you need. You are blessed to have God's Word to delight in and find strength from. Get into it and glean what God wants to teach you.

93 I WILL NEVER FORGET YOUR PRECEPTS, FOR BY THEM YOU HAVE GIVEN ME LIFE.

God's Word brings eternal life. When we read in the Bible concerning where we came from, how we are to live, and where we are going when we die, we're feeding off of God's truth. The question becomes, how do we retain these life-giving precepts that we receive? We retain God's truth by being consumed by His Word. The Lord's precepts will not breed power if we forget them. As humans we often forget what we need to remember, and we remember what we want to forget. In order to get these truths ingrained in our minds, we must be voracious readers of the Word.

If I slack off doing my devotions in the morning, my mind will not rest on the spiritual and my attitude will not be good. If I start the day with reading some verses and praying them in, it completely lifts my countenance.

Ultimately, it's up to you to get into a healthy spiritual pattern by simply making your devotion time a daily habit. Fit the reading of God's Word into your daily schedule so that the Scripture will be planted in your heart and poured out from your life.

94 I AM YOURS, SAVE ME; FOR I HAVE SOUGHT YOUR PRECEPTS.

What a blessing that I am the Lord's. He pursued me, saved me, and now I get to foster my relationship with Him. I find complete comfort in the fact that not only has the Lord saved me, He sustains me. There is no better truth than to know that God set me apart to be a light in this dark world. I am secure in my relationship with Him.

Knowing that we are His gives us determination to seek Him daily through the Scriptures. Our relationship with the Lord should always be our number one priority. Continue to take time to get to know God though His Word; feed yourself with His faithful truths. You are His child and He loves you so much. Ponder His precepts and watch your relationship with the Lord grow deeper and deeper.

95 THE WICKED WAIT FOR ME TO DESTROY ME, BUT I WILL CONSIDER YOUR TESTIMONIES.

The psalmist wasn't worried about his enemies since he considered the testimonies of the Lord. When we read and apply God's decrees, we are deepening our defenses against any and all adversaries. When we base our lives upon the Word of the Lord, we become bold in meeting the challenges in our day-to-day lives. The Word of God is our offensive weapon against the attacks that come against us. We can wield God's Word to fend off temptations that work to take us down. The wicked will remain restrained from afar as we are deep into His Word.

I've learned over and over that the wicked have no power against my almighty God. He is stronger than any of my difficult situations; therefore I have nothing and no one to fear. The psalmist said, "The Lord is my strength and my shield" (Psalm 28:7). When you actively use the Bible as your shield, you are keeping the enemy from penetrating a weak point where he can get a foothold. By applying the Scriptures in your everyday life, you protect yourself against the wiles of the enemy. You have the sword of the Spirit to guard you against temptation and oppression. Use it.

96 I HAVE SEEN THE CONSUMMATION OF ALL PERFECTION, BUT YOUR COMMANDMENT IS EXCEEDINGLY BROAD.

The psalmist had seen some beautiful, amazing things in the world, but he declares God's sure Word is even better. The idea here is that the beautiful things have limitations. They wear out and break down with time. On the other hand, the Word of God endures forever; it is perfectly put together. It tells us the way to live, what to do and how to do it. The Scriptures are not outdated or irrelevant; they are the practical blueprint we get to use for our everyday life. God's Word is perfect and filled with purpose, working on our hearts to refine us.

Before I was a believer I did not know whether I had a purpose or not. I never really thought about the future much or considered deep spiritual truths. It wasn't until I got into God's Word that I realized there is a whole spiritual realm that exists. I found out that God had a call on my life, and my purpose was to walk in His will and live to please Him.

You are limited but God is limitless, and His limitless ways are laid out in His perfect Word. Seek Him daily in the Scriptures and watch the miraculous happen as you live out His commandment.

97 OH, HOW I LOVE YOUR LAW! IT IS MY MEDITATION ALL THE DAY.

This is the third time in Psalm 119 that the psalmist declares he loves God's Word. The language here expresses his passion to think on the Scriptures throughout the day. A person can read the Word of God, but still not be in love with the Word of God. But the truly effective believer will fall in love with God's Word and proclaim it to people that are spiritually lost.

As we hide the Word in our hearts and let it sink into our minds, we have the privilege of meditating on it all day long. Not only do we meditate on God's Word, we get to use it both to fight against temptation and to encourage our own hearts. What a blessing the law of the Lord is. How rich is His Word. How deep is His Word. The more I read the Bible, the more strongly I believe in the Bible and fall in love with it. The Word is truly powerful because it contains the heart and outlook of the Lord. Get into God's Word, not out of obligation but because it will change your life. You'll fall in love with His Word and you'll fall in love with Him. Let God's precepts ignite a passion within your heart and watch God work.

98 YOU, THROUGH YOUR COMMANDMENTS, MAKE ME WISER THAN MY ENEMIES; FOR THEY ARE EVER WITH ME.

The psalmist rightly acknowledges that the Lord's precepts are the way to wisdom. Knowledge is accumulating facts in our minds. Wisdom is applying those facts to our everyday lives. As we get into God's Word, it not only enters our minds; it becomes ingrained in our hearts. We gain knowledge and then use wisdom by acting on His Word.

Please do not strive for wisdom from this world because you will not find it. Ungodly counsel from the world will never lead to real time wisdom. People are longing for something that is genuine and authentic. The truth that they are often unknowingly seeking is found in the Scriptures. So as we gain God's wisdom, we need to share that wisdom with those around us.

God's Word travels in my heart wherever I go. Therefore, if I need to use God's Word to comfort my heart or to comfort the heart of another, it is right there ready to be accessed. If you want wisdom, seek the Lord's leading through His perfect Word—and you will be made wiser than your enemies.

99 I HAVE MORE UNDERSTANDING THAN ALL MY TEACHERS, FOR YOUR TESTIMONIES ARE MY MEDITATION.

It is good to listen to teachers of God's Word, but ultimately meditating on God's Word yourself is where understanding comes from. As we read the Scriptures, we are feeding our spiritual lives and understanding what God is saying to us. No person can tell you what God's calling is for your individual life. It is only through the Lord's Word that we discover God's will.

Going to church, listening to the message, and having fellowship with other believers are ways God confirms what He has already been speaking to us one on one. But we need to have our devotion time in the Bible every day because it feeds our souls. You don't have to rely upon a pastor or spiritual leader to give you the wisdom that you need. You can simply read, enact and depend upon God's Word for divine direction and godly guidance.

100   I UNDERSTAND MORE THAN THE ANCIENTS, BECAUSE I KEEP YOUR PRECEPTS.

The psalmist is not being prideful here, he simply understands that experience and knowledge can only take a person so far. He understands that the ancients, those from times past, may have some profound insights, but the Bible is the fountainhead of wisdom.

Human wisdom does not compare with wisdom from God's precepts. Understanding comes to my heart and life when I am consistently in the Word of the Lord. When I become a doer of God's divine decrees, I am forging ahead in my faith, living according to His ways. The Scriptures seep into my heart and build me up to such an extent that I'm ready for anything the day throws at me. Consequently, I live a carefree, guilt-free life.

If you are lacking understanding, make sure you are meditating on and keeping the Scriptures on a daily basis.

101   I HAVE RESTRAINED MY FEET FROM EVERY EVIL WAY, THAT I MAY KEEP YOUR WORD.

We can understand God's Word better when we keep our lives free of evil. When we begin running the way of the world, we lose sight of how incredibly important God's ways are. Compromise starts slowly and if we're not careful, little by little we will drift from the Lord's decrees. With the Lord's strength we can restrain our feet from evil.

When I was walking in the way of the world, I didn't realize how dark my deeds were—until I came to the light, and then I had to forsake much of what I was doing. It was a blessing to see the Lord change my heart and my desires. I was no longer a slave to sin but was free in Christ, and it all stemmed from reading God's Word. Keep God's Word and walk in His ways and watch as He gives you the wisdom and strength to reject the wiles of the enemy. When temptation comes, the Lord makes a way of escape so that you're not trapped. Take the way of escape and keep evil out of your home. Fill your life with the Word of God so that you'll be built up for battle in this world.

102 I HAVE NOT DEPARTED FROM YOUR JUDGMENTS, FOR YOU YOURSELF HAVE TAUGHT ME.

The Lord speaks to His children through the Scriptures. When we meditate on the Word, we move toward a tight-knit relationship with the Lord. When we lay the Bible aside, we begin to drift away and be distant from the Lord, and our vision for life becomes blurry.

I love going through the Bible line by line because God uses each verse to speak volumes to my heart. I don't want to depart from the Word of God because it leads to a departure from the Lord Himself. James makes it clear in his letter that as we draw near to God, He will draw near to us (James 4:8). Keep seeking the Lord through His Word and in prayer. As you spend time fostering your relationship with your Redeemer, life will be clear. Allow the Lord to teach you, speak to you, and grow your spiritual life to such an extent that there's no hesitation or gap between His leading and your following.

103 HOW SWEET ARE YOUR WORDS TO MY TASTE, SWEETER THAN HONEY TO MY MOUTH!

Honey can be sweet and delicious when devoured. It smells good, tastes good, and has the nutrients to make us healthy and feel good. The psalmist likens the Scriptures to honey. As we meditate upon our Maker's words to us, we realize that God speaks personally to our very hearts. I love reading the Word of God and devouring it on a daily basis. It has the nutrients that I need not just to survive but to thrive and grow stronger in the faith. We hear from the Lord and are connected to the Lord through His Word, and there's nothing sweeter than that.

That the God of the universe takes time for each one of His children is a beautiful reality. Fall in love with the Word of God and meditate upon the treasure of His testimonies. The Scriptures are sweet because they are both personal and powerful. When you constantly get into God's Word, you'll taste the sweetness of the Lord's truth in your life. "Oh, taste and see that the Lord is good; blessed is the man who trusts in Him!" (Psalm 34:8).

104 THROUGH YOUR PRECEPTS I GET UNDERSTANDING; THEREFORE I HATE EVERY FALSE WAY.

Clarity comes from the Creator's words to the world. In order to gain discernment in every situation, we can get into God's Word and the result will be understanding.

I want to know what I'm doing and where I'm going. I don't want to absentmindedly live my life hoping I am making the right decisions. I want to be solely directed by the Lord in every decision I make and every action I take. He knows what's best for me.

To have clarity you simply have to crack open the Bible and see what God has for you. The moment you look to the world for direction is the moment you are led astray by every false way. Stick to the truth in order to hear from the Lord. Open His Word and gain understanding concerning life and godliness. The more you peer into the Bible, the more you'll hate every false way and renounce those actions you used to desire. Let the Word of God refine you, knock off those rough edges, and work in your heart from the inside out.

105 YOUR WORD IS A LAMP TO MY FEET AND A LIGHT TO MY PATH.

God's Word illuminates our path in life. One of the most confusing places to be is where there's just darkness and no light in our lives. We can thank the Lord that our God-given path is lit up by His perfect Word. I don't want to walk in the dark or navigate in this dim world without God's Word. I want to know where my destination is. I desire to embrace my calling and trust in the plan that God has for me.

The times in my Christian life when I was confused were the times that I was not in the Lord's Word. I wasn't digging into it and allowing it to light up my divine path.

God's plan for you will be clear as you simply get into His Word and let it light up the path in front of you. He will give you both your direction and your destination. He may not illuminate the entire way at once but He will shine His light before you so you can take those steps of faith knowing the Lord is leading. Trust Him!

106 I HAVE SWORN AND CONFIRMED THAT I WILL KEEP YOUR RIGHTEOUS JUDGMENTS.

In this verse we can see a determination and resolve by the psalmist to keep God's Word. We can't passively hope that we'll keep God's Word, we have to proactively keep the faith. If we just let things happen, then we will end up astray and far from where God wants us.

Anytime in my life where I failed to take God's Word seriously, those were the moments that I felt far from Him. I've come to realize that the more I seek God by reading the Scriptures, the more He speaks to me. I don't ever want to stray from where the Lord wants me in life. I want to do what He's called me to do with total confidence in Him.

You can purpose in your heart to seek the Lord through His Word and follow His ways. He wants to meet you where you're at in your life. The determination to seek the Lord comes from implementing healthy spiritual habits on a daily basis. May your devotion time in God's Word be a process that you put into place steadily. If you haven't already, start today.

107 I AM AFFLICTED VERY MUCH; REVIVE ME, O LORD, ACCORDING TO YOUR WORD.

Life can definitely wear on us as we go through our day-to-day regimen. We can get weary and worn out, exhausted and exasperated. There are moments where we feel like we cannot get through one more day. The psalmist was struggling at this point; yet he clearly knew the key to being revived. The source of our revival and rejuvenation is God's Word.

Countless times when I have felt like I had nothing left in me, I cracked open God's Word, read the Scriptures and got instantly revived. My heart awakens and my eyes are opened. I remember and realize what true life is about. God's Word is the source of spiritual strength and the avenue to be on fire for the Lord. When you are feeling the negative effects of life, grab your Bible and just let His words sink into your weary soul. You'll end up revived and refreshed, ready for whatever life throws at you.

108 ACCEPT, I PRAY, THE FREEWILL OFFERINGS OF MY MOUTH, O LORD, AND TEACH ME YOUR JUDGMENTS.

Our words matter. With our words we pray to the Lord and daily seek Him with our mouths. We praise God with our words and worship Him as He is worthy to be praised. We get to use our words to build up other believers and teach the Scriptures. As we read God's Word, it causes us to see life clearly and it makes us realize that our words have weight.

I don't want to use my words to break people down or discourage others. I want to use my words to build people up and encourage their hearts. My words alone are completely insufficient. The way to use our words for the Lord is to relay His Word to others. You know some verses by heart and you may have read the Bible for years. You know enough of the Scriptures to tell others about what you've learned. Make it a healthy habit to read God's Word and share what you've read to at least one person every day. I believe you'll find this action to be so impactful to you and to those you share God's Word with.

109 MY LIFE IS CONTINUALLY IN MY HAND, YET I DO NOT FORGET YOUR LAW.

The life of the psalmist was constantly in danger. He had adversaries who wanted to see him fail. By remembering God's Word he stood strong against such forces.

In the face of danger, the Scriptures give us the assurance we truly need to fight every battle with faith. I've had some life circumstances come against me and I am so thankful the Lord brought specific verses to my mind during those times of trouble. God's Word acts as a shield to protect us from the onslaught of unexpected difficulties.

As you face seemingly impossible situations in your life, think on what God's Word says. Actively use the Scriptures to curb any onslaught of problems. Use God's Word as a defensive weapon in the face of unsettling circumstances. Situations can come against us, but we have the truth to tame our hearts in the midst of tumultuous times.

110 THE WICKED HAVE LAID A SNARE FOR ME, YET I HAVE NOT STRAYED FROM YOUR PRECEPTS.

We not only face physical danger; we also face spiritual danger. As believers we have unseen enemies all around us rallying together to try to tear us apart. Yet, the darkness cannot cause us to crash as long as we're sticking to the Scriptures. If we do stray from the precepts of the Lord, it may be due to the lures and traps the enemy sets for us. There have been times in my Christian life where I have been too weak to fight those unseen enemies of discouragement. I look back and realize the reason I had stumbled was because I had strayed from God's Word and was far away from fellowship. I had begun distancing myself from the things of the Lord. The way I was anchored back to the Lord was to get back on the boat which was captained by God. In order to return to my relationship with the Lord, I needed to get back into His instruction manual, His Word. If you have drifted a bit from the things of God, get back on the boat. If you have distanced yourself from fellowship, get reconnected with like-minded believers. The way you can fight against unseen forces is to wield your sword which is God's Word.

111 YOUR TESTIMONIES I HAVE TAKEN AS A HERITAGE FOREVER, FOR THEY ARE THE REJOICING OF MY HEART.

The psalmist's heritage, his goal and main focus, was to get into and keep the Word of God. When we make the Scriptures the focus of our lives, we will be on track to exponentially grow in our faith.

When I do my daily devotions, it brings joy to my heart because I know I'm being spoken to by the living God! This fact gives me such peace and gratefulness. It is so mind-blowing that the God of the universe connects with His children individually as we read through the Bible. God wants to speak to you on a consistent basis. As you open the Scriptures, pray and your eyes will be opened to the Lord's ways. You will hear His voice and life will become clear. God's heart can be seen in the pages of Scripture. The more you get into the Lord's Word, the clearer your divine direction will become.

112 I HAVE INCLINED MY HEART TO PERFORM YOUR STATUTES FOREVER, TO THE VERY END.

The psalmist's desire was to have a heart that was bent toward the Lord. He understood that obeying the Lord doesn't start with actions, but it begins in the heart. I love hearing the statutes of God and then putting them into action. Obeying God is not a burden, it is a great blessing and it leads to bountiful living. Those times where I did not adhere to God's statutes were the times where I was so lost and so disoriented. When I ran back to the Lord's way, I realized how good it is to walk on God's path for me. I want to finish this race of faith well, and in order to do so I need to cling to God's Word. As you live to please the Lord, may God's Word penetrate your heart and affect your life. As you are obedient to Him, you'll enter into His will and the result will be radical blessings to the very end.

113 I HATE THE DOUBLE-MINDED, BUT I LOVE YOUR LAW.

It can be so frustrating dealing with those who are inconsistent in their walk with the Lord. They know about God, but they are not fully committed to following Him. This psalm contrasts between those who are not fully invested in the Lord and those who are fully invested in the Lord. It is thought that the psalmist himself struggled with fully following the Lord. All throughout Psalm 119 he prays in desperation to keep the Word of the Lord.

I've found that I need to stay desperate for God's Word. When I begin to think I can walk with God in my own strength, I become inconsistent in my Christian life. I love God's Word and I know I can keep it with His strength and His leading. Consistency is the key to a strong spiritual life. A daily habit of seeking God through His Word is what will keep you on the road of God's will. Don't forsake your devotion time. Carve out a time where you can just read the Bible and pray His Word into your heart.

114 YOU ARE MY HIDING PLACE AND MY SHIELD; I HOPE IN YOUR WORD.

No matter what external situations we face, we can always find solace in our Savior. God is the One who completely protects us and shields us from the discouragement of the world. As the Lord holds us up and we hope in His truth, our countenance will be lifted up. *Hope* here means "a hope that is sure and unwavering." God is our hiding place; He shields us from those unhealthy carnal temptations that can potentially take us out.

I am so thankful that I can be confident that the Lord is shielding me from being lured away from the lusts of the flesh. When you base your life on God's Word, you are building your life on a solid foundation with impenetrable walls, safeguarding you from all the darts of the enemy. Continue to find your solace in your Savior and never stop hoping in God's perfect Word.

115 DEPART FROM ME, YOU EVILDOERS, FOR I WILL KEEP THE COMMANDMENTS OF MY GOD!

The people we decide to surround ourselves with will influence the actions that we take. If we constantly hang out with people who might potentially pull us away from God, it's time to make some changes. Now we are not to reject people and abandon them. But we are to make wise choices when it comes to the voices we let into our lives. We need to be smart about this.

As we gather together with believers who love the Lord, we are building our soul up in order to be an influence for the good, not evil. No matter what evil tries to invade our lives, may we keep God's Word and not be moved away from God's ways.

I don't want to ever be moved away from living a life that is well pleasing to God. If I'm not diligently and consistently doing my devotion time in the Bible, then I can easily be moved away from God's ways. Stay close to the Lord through His Word and through prayer.

Use God's wisdom when it comes to whose voices you let into your life. Separate yourself from evil, yet be a light to those who are lost. Stay strong in the Lord and keep your heart bent toward Him.

116 UPHOLD ME ACCORDING TO YOUR WORD, THAT I MAY LIVE; AND DO NOT LET ME BE ASHAMED OF MY HOPE.

The Lord upholds us in this life by His Word. How many times have we been struggling and suffering—only to find solace in the Word of God? Every time we open the pages of Scripture we are reminded of our purpose in life. We are reminded of who we are in Christ. Our identity becomes clear and life makes sense. As we sink into the Word of God, we see the Bible as a blueprint for our lives.

There is absolutely no reason to be ashamed of the words or ways of the Lord. The hope that God's Word gives is a sure hope that helps us to live passionately for the Lord. As I put Him first, my priorities line up perfectly. I know the Lord is upholding me every day, all the time. God wants you to live boldly for Him. There is no place for timidity. The way to live boldly is to feed your faith through His Word. Remember that it has brought life to you and it can bring life to the hearers.

117 HOLD ME UP, AND I SHALL BE SAFE, AND I SHALL OBSERVE YOUR STATUTES CONTINUALLY.

It's a comforting fact that the Lord keeps us safe in this unsafe world. Many dangers attempt to take us away from the Lord and many temptations work to tear us away from the faith. The enemy wants people to think that walking by faith is a silly myth. He wants to move anyone remotely passionate about the Lord away from God.

There is a major connection between staying safe and being in God's Word. When I consistently dig into the Bible, the truth permeates my mind and keeps me grounded so I can't be lured away by sin. I know that it's imperative for me to keep my eyes upon the Word of God to hold the correct perspective on life. As you stay in the Scriptures, you'll be safe from any spiritual harm. In other words, no darkness can touch your heart and the enemy can have no control over your mind. You are safe in the Father's arms. Stay in God's Word and continually walk with Him.

118 YOU REJECT ALL THOSE WHO STRAY FROM YOUR STATUTES, FOR THEIR DECEIT IS FALSEHOOD.

The word *statutes* actually refers to the fact that God's judgment is based on our adherence to His Word. The Lord is a just judge and those who hear His Word and accept Him will see God do amazing works. Those who reject His Word, He rejects. This is why it is so important to read and receive God's Word.

We are called not only to read but to give out God's Word. Let people know the power of God as we share the Scriptures. May we pray for those who stray from the statutes of the Lord. Seek the Lord through His Word and stay in the center of God's will. There is deceit and falsehood all around us and the way to guard against those things is to keep our eyes upon the statutes of our God.

119 YOU PUT AWAY ALL THE WICKED OF THE EARTH LIKE DROSS; THEREFORE I LOVE YOUR TESTIMONIES.

We can be assured that our God is completely just. The wicked cannot touch the soul of those who walk with God. We have nothing to fear and every reason to be confident. The Lord is our protector from all things evil. He is our shield in the midst of this shady and sketchy world. God's testimonies have shown over and over again that the wicked, who are against the Lord, have no power. Those who mock God do not understand that they are ridiculing the One who created and sustains them.

Before I was a believer, I mocked God by default. I just laughed at all things spiritual and I really didn't care about anything related to the Lord. When I got saved, I realized the true state of my heart. I was wicked and I needed to repent and walk with God! In my fallen state the Lord spared me and changed my life. Don't take for granted the life that God has given you. At one time you were an enemy of the Lord by default, but now you are a child of God. He takes care of all His children and He will continue to take care of you.

120 MY FLESH TREMBLES FOR FEAR OF YOU, AND I AM AFRAID OF YOUR JUDGMENTS.

There is such a thing as a healthy fear of the Lord. Fearing the Lord means to stand in awe and amazement as we worship Him. Fearing the Lord causes us to stand in adoration of our almighty God. How we view the Lord will affect the way we live for Him. If we see God in a casual manner, we will live in an irreverent way. If we see God in a reverent manner and take the Scriptures seriously, we will have the right view of God.

There is such a lack of reverence for the Lord in this lost world. People don't take Him at His Word anymore and actually mock God. Since I've been a believer, I have learned how amazing and powerful the Lord is. This causes me to revere the Lord and take His Word seriously! I've seen the miraculous feats that God has done in my life and it truly amazes me. Make sure you have the correct view of the Lord. When you have reverence for the Lord, you'll live to please Him. Know that God uses His power to equip you to live for His purposes. Stand in awe of your almighty God and watch Him do great things in your life.

121 I HAVE DONE JUSTICE AND RIGHTEOUSNESS; DO NOT LEAVE ME TO MY OPPRESSORS.

The psalmist sought God's Word and lived righteously for the Lord. The way we are called to live is clearly outlined in the Scriptures. The psalmist prayed that the Lord wouldn't leave him to his oppressors. Sometimes those that are against us can scare us. In those instances, the Lord's Word is what calms our heart and lifts our countenance. God can and often does tame our tumultuous hearts. The Lord reassures us over and over again that He is our shield and our protection.

There have been some intense times in my life where I was painfully afraid. I cried out to the Lord and He met me exactly where I was at. He reminded me of Scriptures that would protect my mind and shield my heart. As you adhere to God's Word, He will give you the peace in your heart that you need. There's nothing more comforting than the Lord's reassuring words. Let God's Word be integrated into your mind and immersed into your heart. His Words will give you all you need to get through every single day with joy.

122 BE SURETY FOR YOUR SERVANT FOR GOOD; DO NOT LET THE PROUD OPPRESS ME.

As the Lord is our defender, it will be impossible for the proud to oppress us. The enemy wants us to be weighed down and taken out of any God-led actions. Our oppressors want to stop us living for the Lord. Yet God protects us and He defends us from those who come against us. Therefore, there is no need to worry or wonder if we're going to make it through. With the Lord as our defense and His Word as our weapon, we are completely safe.

Just like the psalmist, we need to be honest when our hearts are in desperation. We can come to the Lord for help and He will meet our need. There have been numerous times that I have felt like the oppression of this world could overtake me. During those tumultuous times I sought God in prayer and opened His Word, and the result was freedom. You have nothing to fear in this life for the Lord is your surety—He is your strong tower, your hiding place. Therefore, no oppression can ever overtake you.

123 MY EYES FAIL FROM SEEKING YOUR SALVATION AND YOUR RIGHTEOUS WORD.

This verse demonstrates the major commitment that the psalmist had to read God's Word regularly. He was in the Scriptures so much that his vision became blurry! Not only was he in God's Word regularly, he also valued and was blessed by the salvation given by God's Word. This verse demonstrates the right order—faith comes before our experiences. We have faith in God's Word even if we don't feel anything. There are times where we may go through dry spells and we don't *feel* that God is near. During those times we need to have faith in what God has already promised.

I've had major desert seasons where the Lord seemed distant. But as I stayed in the Scriptures, I was reminded that He is right there with me. Seek the Lord through His Word on a daily basis and allow Him to speak to you. Soak in the Scriptures and see what God would have you do. The Scriptures speak to your life in a very personal way and the Bible outlines God's will for you. Read His Word until your vision blurs. Be hungry for God's Word and let it grow your heart for the Lord.

124 DEAL WITH YOUR SERVANT ACCORDING TO YOUR MERCY, AND TEACH ME YOUR STATUTES.

A constant theme in Scripture is God's mercy. The more we read the Word of the Lord, the more we come to realize God is so incredibly merciful toward His children! He has every right to take us out, but because of His mercy we are still here. *Mercy* basically means "we don't get what we deserve." As fallen and sin-ridden human beings, we deserve death, darkness and destruction. I realize this sounds so incredibly harsh and intense. But God's mercy turns death into life, darkness into light, and destruction into deliverance. I am blown away that God's mercies are new every morning (Lamentations 3:23). His mercies are new because we need to live a life of freedom and forgiveness. God's mercy gives me a glimpse into the character of God.

As I delve into the Scriptures, I realize over and over again that God's mercies are there for me. Remember and revel in the fact that God has mercy on you. God's mercy will cover you and console you during those rough times where you feel like you can't do anything right. The fact is, you really can't! We are all failures. Praise God, every morning the Lord fills us with faith and mercy.

125 I AM YOUR SERVANT; GIVE ME UNDERSTANDING, THAT I MAY KNOW YOUR TESTIMONIES.

We serve an amazing God who desires that we know His Word. The more we get to know His Word, the more we flourish in the faith. As we grow closer to God, we learn that living to please Him is what life is about. When I was a new Christian I was avidly reading the Bible. I could not get enough of the Gospel of Matthew, the first book I began reading when someone bought me a Bible. I learned about the Lord's heart, the Lord's ways, and the Lord's desires. I wanted nothing more than to glean from God's heart so my heart would bend toward His.

I began to understand His will and calling for my life. I began to serve the Lord practically and tangibly, sweeping the leaves off of the front walkway, and attending church diligently. I absolutely loved serving the Lord in whatever way I could, and it all started with understanding God's Word. As you read the Scriptures you'll come to realize what a major blessing it is to practically serve the Lord; to do everything as unto the Lord and to live fully for the Lord. Get into His Word, soak it in and let it change your heart and life.

126 IT IS TIME FOR YOU TO ACT, O LORD, FOR THEY HAVE REGARDED YOUR LAW AS VOID.

There have been and there always will be those who mock the things of God and think spiritual things are not real. They will reject Him over and over again. We can take comfort in the fact that God is a just judge. The pressure is off of us because we don't judge anyone's soul, it is the Lord who is in charge. All we are called to do is love God, love others, and spread the truth. He does the work and makes things right. The Holy Spirit actually brings conviction to unbelievers who think there is no God.

I'll never forget how before I was a believer, I definitely felt convicted by actions I took and words I said against God and Christianity. When people shared the gospel with me, I realized I needed to get right with God and grow close to the Lord.

Time is too short to let life fly by without living for your God-given purpose. You can be a beacon of light to those who reject the Lord and who think faith is foolishness. If they are still breathing, there is still opportunity for them to get saved and begin their journey with God. Sometimes those people who hate Christianity may be the ones who are the closest to accepting Christ. Keep shining your light in this dim world.

127 THEREFORE I LOVE YOUR COMMANDMENTS MORE THAN GOLD, YES, THAN FINE GOLD!

As the enemies of God rejected the Word of God, it caused the psalmist to double down on his love of the Scriptures. He found that his riches were not in gold or silver but in God's perfect Word. I love going through God's Word on a regular basis because it establishes my faith and it causes me to see how good God is. He is so good that He gives salvation, and a hope and future that is beautiful. I've seen materially poor people that are so incredibly strong in the Lord and I've seen well off people who are destitute in spiritual things.

I treasure God's Word and I always will. Since my eyes were opened to the riches of God's Word, I cling to them for life, clarity and direction. Money cannot build a godly character into your life. Worldly riches can do nothing to feed your soul and direct your eyes to a tight-knit relationship with God. Seek Him as you read His Word, fall in love with His commandments and you'll realize how rich you actually are.

128 THEREFORE ALL YOUR PRECEPTS CONCERNING ALL THINGS I CONSIDER TO BE RIGHT; I HATE EVERY FALSE WAY.

All things that pertain to life and godliness are in God's Word; and therefore, we can completely trust its precepts. God's precepts are perfect and we can count on God's counsel. Second Samuel 7:28 says, "Now, O Lord GOD, You are God, and Your words are truth."

Before I began walking with the Lord, I believed all kinds of lies about life. I was attempting to be led by my carnal desires which never led to anything good; I ended up empty and alone. Reading God's Word quickly taught me that the Bible is a book of answers, not questions. Every one of life's deep questions were answered as I simply read the Bible. Not only did I realize the Word of God was truth, I found out that the truth really does lead to freedom. As you delve into the decrees of the Lord, it will affect your life and fill your heart. The truth from God is living and life-transforming. Let God's words seep into the deepest part of your heart and change you from the inside out.

129 YOUR TESTIMONIES ARE WONDERFUL; THEREFORE MY SOUL KEEPS THEM.

We can revel in the amazingness of God's Word because His testimonies are wonderful. It's not out of strict obligation to keep God's Word, it's a joy! When we adhere to God's Word, we walk through life guilt-free. We can fall in love with reading the Scriptures because in them the Lord gives us all we need to resist those temptations that attempt to tear us down.

When I'm out of God's Word, I struggle so much. I become discouraged and disgruntled. My attitude goes from blessed to bad. I lose perspective. But when I start my day off with my devotion time, my whole perspective, attitude and countenance change. I remember my purpose in life and the reason I have breath in my lungs. I realize that God's will is why I exist on this earth. I'm called to take in God's Word and then give out God's Word.

You are blessed to have the whole counsel of God to pull from. You'll find such joy in gleaning from the precepts that are God-breathed. Seeking the Lord will heighten your countenance, improve your attitude and remind you what your calling on this earth is. You are not made for this world; you are made for heaven and you are in this world to spread God's beautiful Word.

130 THE ENTRANCE OF YOUR WORDS GIVES LIGHT; IT GIVES UNDERSTANDING TO THE SIMPLE.

God's Word illuminates the path that God has us walking on. The Jews were Bedouins living in tents. In order for light to come in, they would open the flap of their tents. It was a necessity so the occupants could see. It's the same with the Scriptures. When we open God's Word, the truth illuminates our way and makes our calling clear. We attain understanding when the precepts of the Lord are in front of us.

I lived for years in a dim world not knowing truth, with absolutely no direction and no clear purpose. I was lost and confused. I followed the desires of my own heart and tried to pave my own way. Not until I started reading God's Word did I realize that I had a purpose and calling in life from God Himself. The emptiness began to be filled and my confusion transformed into clarity as the light of God's Word directed my path. God has a calling for you as well. He wants to make clear to you what He's calling you to. Open up His Word and let it reveal His will to your life. As you seek Him in the Scriptures, your eyes will be opened to His works and His ways.

131 I OPENED MY MOUTH AND PANTED, FOR I LONGED FOR YOUR COMMANDMENTS.

Panting means "to desire." What we see is the desperateness of the psalmist for the Word of God. Being desperate is not a bad thing when the focal point is God's Word. When we truly understand that we *need* the statutes of God, we will saturate ourselves with the truth and set our feet on the right path. Jesus spoke about how we will be filled when we hunger and thirst for righteousness (Matthew 5:6). The more I delve into God's decrees, the more I am filled and the more I desire even more of the Scriptures. Spiritual growth stems from the statutes of the Lord and emanates from His eternal Word. As you desire to grow deeper in your relationship with God, make sure to develop the healthy spiritual habit of doing a devotion time. Carve out a time every day where you can seek God and get His Word into your heart. "As the deer pants for the water brooks, so pants my soul for You, O God. My soul thirsts for God, for the living God" (Psalm 42:1-2).

132 LOOK UPON ME AND BE MERCIFUL TO ME, AS YOUR CUSTOM IS TOWARD THOSE WHO LOVE YOUR NAME.

God sees us and cares about us. He loves us so much that He lavishes His mercy upon us. In other words, God doesn't give us what we deserve for being sinners. God's heart is so good toward His children, it leaves us overwhelmed. The Lord's goodness causes us to love His name more and more each day. I am astounded by the heart of God as I go through His Word. After all these years my jaw still drops as I get reminded how good He is. When we look at our own hearts, we may be left discouraged. When we look at God's heart, we can be encouraged and lifted up.

You are blessed when you follow the God who created you. He loves you and has mercy upon you. He cares about what you go through. He listens. He won't turn His back on you. When you fail, He is faithful. When you stumble, He will catch you. The love that you have for God will increase as you read His Word and know His heart.

133 DIRECT MY STEPS BY YOUR WORD, AND LET NO INIQUITY HAVE DOMINION OVER ME.

Our steps are directed, either by things of the world or by God's Word. When we allow the world's ways to grab a hold of us, our conscience will become seared as sin dictates our decision-making. When we are directed by God's Word, we will be on His divine path for us. Self-leading can result in an ungodly destination. We have to stick to God's Word and let Him lead our daily lives.

I don't want to let the world dictate my destination. I don't want to be directed to fleshly, surface level goals. I want the Lord to direct my steps because He knows exactly where I need to be. Let the Lord's Word lead you today. He will light up your path and lead you to the exact destination you are supposed to be at. When you seek God through His Word, He will speak to you and direct your steps. Keep seeking the Lord in the Scriptures and sin will not have a foothold on your life. Being consistently in God's precepts will block any temptation from progressing into sin.

134 REDEEM ME FROM THE OPPRESSION OF MAN, THAT I MAY KEEP YOUR PRECEPTS.

The psalmist didn't just want freedom for himself, he wanted freedom to be able to keep God's precepts. Sometimes the actions of others attempt to stunt our spiritual growth and put a stop to our spiritual progress. Let it not be so. The Lord is the One who paves the way for our walk in this life. As we seek Him, there will be those who desire to see us walk away from our almighty God. There have been people in my life who have tried to discourage me from following the Lord. Yet, what they don't realize is how amazing it is to foster a solid relationship with the Father. There is nothing like living for the Lord and adhering to His Word. The longer I walk with the Lord, the more in awe I become of what He's done for me and who He is! As long as you are sticking to the Scriptures, no oppressors can move you away from your almighty God. Stay strong by daily digging into God's Word. Nothing can impede your spiritual development as long as you are seeking your loving Lord.

135 MAKE YOUR FACE SHINE UPON YOUR SERVANT, AND TEACH ME YOUR STATUTES.

To have God's face shining upon His children has everything to do with knowing His peace. The peace that comes from the Lord is a peace that so many people in this world are searching for. As we get into God's Word, pray to Him and seek Him, we begin to experience His peace. And what results is a heart of rest. In this chaotic and unsure world, remember that the Lord is our source of permanent peace. Focus on the Father and let His face shine upon you (Numbers 6:25).

As I read God's Word, I continue to learn that God's peace is genuine and real. I've attempted to search for peace before I began walking with the Lord and I could never find it. Only in knowing and walking with the Lord is there any real life-changing peace. You are not meant to live a chaotic and worrisome existence. God wants to fill you with His peace and His rest. He wants to shine His face upon you in this dim world. Let Him in and get into His Word. The result is true rest.

136 RIVERS OF WATER RUN DOWN FROM MY EYES, BECAUSE MEN DO NOT KEEP YOUR LAW.

The psalmist had sorrow and compassion for those who rejected God's Law. He cared about the souls who were lost and astray. He didn't sorrow for himself; he sorrowed for others who were far from God. The Lord loves those who are lost and He grieves when people are not walking according to His ways. I was lost for so long. It was a confusing and stressful time. When I began walking with the Lord and adhering to His ways, everything in life became clear. When I was saved, I then began having a heart for other lost souls who were searching for truth. The Lord gives us a heart for the lost because they need to be found; they need to know truth.

When you get to know God, you'll want to reach the lost with His love. When you realize the huge heart the Lord has for people, you will want to let them know who God is and what He's done for them. Pray for boldness and step out in faith to reach those who are lost and alone. Have compassion upon the multitudes like Jesus did, and spread the gospel as far and wide as you can. When we spread the truth and people are saved, God is pleased.

137 RIGHTEOUS ARE YOU, O LORD, AND UPRIGHT ARE YOUR JUDGMENTS.

The Lord is a just judge and His ways are perfect. He doesn't make mistakes and He is completely fair. No one on earth is like that.

We are not called to be the judge of souls; that is God's job. We are called to share the truth in love to this lost world. In order for me to share truth, I have to be in the truth from day to day. I can't give out what I haven't taken in. As I read through the Scriptures, the Lord speaks to me and I am able to then go out and share His truth with this world that needs it so desperately. You have that same opportunity. Every day you can decide to open God's Word and let it seep into your heart and mind. You can then get out there and share what He has spoken to you. It's not a burden to share the truth;

it is truly a blessing. The more we read God's Word, the more we get to know that He is perfectly righteous in his judgments.

138 YOUR TESTIMONIES, WHICH YOU HAVE COMMANDED, ARE RIGHTEOUS AND VERY FAITHFUL.

God's testimonies tell us the truth about who God is. Many people want to know who God is but they don't use the Bible as their source of that knowledge. I believe with all my heart that His testimonies are righteous. God knows best. He always has and He always will. The Lord is the One who literally knows everything.

We can be so encouraged to know that what God tells us to do as believers is for our good. I know that God wants the best for me, and the best for me is to walk in His will. As I continue in God's encouraging Word, He makes it so incredibly transparent where He wants me to go.

You have the privilege of daily walking with the Lord and heeding His ways. As you continue to be in line with the Lord's testimonies, you'll realize how good God is. He has a huge heart of love for each one of His children. He knows every situation you face and He is there to guide you by His perfect Word. He is faithful to direct you to your correct destination.

139 MY ZEAL HAS CONSUMED ME, BECAUSE MY ENEMIES HAVE FORGOTTEN YOUR WORDS.

The psalmist made sure to hold high the Word of God even if his enemies did not. He didn't let them dictate his actions or passions. We need to stick to the

Scriptures no matter what for they bring clarity to our life and our calling. May we be zealous in our reading of the Word and find fulfillment in reading what God has written.

Some people hear God's Word but very quickly they forget what they've heard or they don't take it seriously. I believe wholeheartedly that the words contained in the Bible are life-changing. My mind and heart have been transformed by the testimonies from the Word of the Lord. It blows me away that the Scriptures can have such a powerful impact on those who read them with an open heart. I pray that you'd be zealous for the Word of the Lord; that you'd not let anything or anyone stop you from allowing the truth of the Bible to take residence in your heart. Seek the Lord through His Word and hear His voice speak to your very situation.

140 YOUR WORD IS VERY PURE; THEREFORE YOUR SERVANT LOVES IT.

The Word of God is completely reliable because it is God-breathed. In other words, the Holy Spirit inspired the writers of the Bible to pen His perfect precepts, making it so pure. Not only is the Word pure, it also purifies us! As we read through the Scriptures, our hearts desire to be pure as we walk down the path of God's will. We are far from perfect but we are being perfected by the Lord's radical work. We're all works in progress and we can thank God that He doesn't give up on us.

I am so blessed that the Scriptures are completely reliable and relevant to our lives in this century. This is the reason I had it on my heart to write this devotional. I desire to see people get into God's Word and grow spiritually. I believe one of my directives as a pastor is to encourage people to read and stay in the Word of the Lord. I know for a fact that as you read the words of the Lord, you will flourish in your faith, your spiritual life will soar, and you'll stand firm on the promises of God. Get into God's Word and let Him do amazing heart work in you. "Every word of God is pure; He is a shield to those who put their trust in Him" (Proverbs 30:5).

141 I AM SMALL AND DESPISED, YET I DO NOT FORGET YOUR PRECEPTS.

The psalmist felt small and insignificant in life. He did not feel worthy or of much worth at this moment. Yet, I love what he follows this statement with—"I do not forget Your precepts." The promises of God reminded him that he was significant in God's eyes.

The Lord loves us so much and He wants us to stay in line with His will. He keeps us safe and fills us with boldness so we can be used by Him. I am loved by God and He would never see me as insignificant or useless. Sometimes others make us feel insignificant and worth little. Sometimes our failures make us feel insignificant and downcast. But God makes you and I feel loved, accepted, cherished and adored. God loves you more than ever. You are His workmanship. You are His poem. He sees what you're going through and He truly cares. He is close to you and He wants to lead you out of love.

142 YOUR RIGHTEOUSNESS IS AN EVERLASTING RIGHTEOUSNESS, AND YOUR LAW IS TRUTH.

God has been and always will be righteous; He is a just judge who gives a perfect and fair verdict. He is the constant in our sometimes inconsistent lives. The world promotes moral relativism, which says whatever makes you feel good, that's fine to do. Yet, God clearly outlines in His Word the way in which we are to live—not because He is restricting us but because He wants us to have fullness of joy. True joy comes from walking in God's testimonies. The law of the Lord is truth. I love walking in the ways of the Lord because He knows how I need to live in order to have freedom. Life as a believer is so amazing I can't imagine life without Him. You are blessed to be a follower of Jesus. God is righteous and He knows you and He loves you. His Word is truth, and as you grow in His strength, you can adhere to His truth and the freedom that you have in Him!

143 TROUBLE AND ANGUISH HAVE OVERTAKEN ME, YET YOUR COMMANDMENTS ARE MY DELIGHTS.

We all face heart-wrenching trials in life at one time or another. We've gone through some situations that we wouldn't wish for anyone to go through. We've faced hardships that have threatened to take us out. The trials in our lives are real. The storms that we have experienced, or are bound to experience, are vicious and intense. Yet, even in the most difficult and unpredictable times, God's Word stays the same and we can delight in it. We can find joy in God's Word even when circumstances are less than favorable. God's Word lifts our countenance like nothing else in this world.

I have found comfort countless times as I read what the Lord has to say in the midst of a tough situation. God's perfect Word will get you through. His Word will give you the promises that fill you with hope in the midst of major problems. Stay in God's Word and your perspective will go from defeat to deliverance.

144 THE RIGHTEOUSNESS OF YOUR TESTIMONIES IS EVERLASTING; GIVE ME UNDERSTANDING, AND I SHALL LIVE.

The psalmist truly understood the Bible's internal character. God's Word is always consistent as a whole. It is good for us to ask God to give us understanding as we read through the Scriptures. Some people don't put much importance in doing daily devotions. I think this is a huge mistake because the more we're in the Word, the clearer life becomes. The more I'm in the Scriptures, the more I realize what my specific calling in life is and the more I understand His purposes for me. I want to get to know God's heart!

I encourage you to fall in love with the Word of the Lord and stay in it continually. It will keep you grounded and established in the truth. It will define your roles in life and it will give you a clear glimpse of God's heart. Let the Lord's Word penetrate your heart and infiltrate your mind so you can have a calm and a clarity that this world will never bring.

FALLING IN LOVE WITH GOD'S WORD

145 I CRY OUT WITH MY WHOLE HEART; HEAR ME, O LORD! I WILL KEEP YOUR STATUTES.

It is actually a blessing to be desperate for the Lord. When we cry out to God, we demonstrate our dependence upon Him. We don't seek help from people first, we seek the Lord for help through His Word. Going to God first is the action every believer is called to take. So many times when we are going through conflict, seeking the Lord comes last on our list. We'd do well to seek God first in every one of our situations. Not only are we called to seek the Lord, we are called to seek the Lord with our whole heart. The beautiful thing is that the Lord hears our cries and cares about what we face.

I've gone through my fair share of trials and heartaches. Every time I went through some kind of storm and I cried out to the Lord, He faithfully met me right where I was at. He helped me and gave me hope to continue to move forward. Seek God in every one of your situations. He hears you and He cares. Dig into His Word and open your heart to allow Him to speak straight to your situation. God loves you so much and I believe He wants you to come to Him daily and lay your problems and trials at His feet.

146 I CRY OUT TO YOU; SAVE ME, AND I WILL KEEP YOUR TESTIMONIES.

Why do we cry out to the Lord? The reason is because we don't want to pretend that we can do life on our own. It is the Lord who we lean upon, who holds us up, and who paves our path. He is who we look to on a daily basis! We don't look to ourselves or others for true help, we run to the Lord knowing that He is more than capable of lifting us up when we are down. As we seek the Lord through His Word, we realize He is the only One who will never let us down. He will never break a promise. And we keep His testimonies not because we have to, but because we want to. God has done so much in my life! He saved me from myself and He has grown me in ways I never thought possible. God is so good that I sometimes have no words to express how grateful I am. Thank the Lord for your salvation. Thank the Lord for always coming through in every one of your circumstances. Thank God for His Word and the fact that you get to freely read it and grow from it. Have a grateful heart today!

147 I RISE BEFORE THE DAWNING OF THE MORNING, AND CRY FOR HELP; I HOPE IN YOUR WORD.

It is so amazing to hope in God's Word. Many people hope in so many things and they are let down and disappointed. The hope that we have from God's Word never leads to disappointment; it always leads to clarity. It makes us realize that God always comes through. We have the opportunity to wake up every morning and seek the Lord through prayer and through the Scriptures.

I personally love seeking God early in the morning. It is quiet and I can read God's Word without any distraction. I easily get distracted throughout the day by the noise from the world. To me, to have some quiet time to just glean from the Lord is amazing. Every time you get into God's Word He wants to speak to you. He wants to give you comfort in the midst of your chaos. He wants to give you peace in the midst of your problems. God is faithful to you and He always will be. Trust in Him and find those times where you can sit quietly and just soak in His Word.

148 MY EYES ARE AWAKE THROUGH THE NIGHT WATCHES, THAT I MAY MEDITATE ON YOUR WORD.

Not only did the psalmist rise early in the morning to read God's Word, He also stayed up through the night to meditate on it. It is a good sign when we can't get enough of the Scriptures. When we hunger and thirst for truth and dig into the source of truth—God's Word—it will increase our craving for the ways of God. What a blessing to be able to meditate on and ponder God's Word on a regular basis. Life has never been as clear as when I am consistently digging into the well of God's Word. It's beautiful to read a verse in the morning at home and meditate upon that verse the rest of the day. To let what God has spoken sink in and set your heart right is an amazing experience. If you aren't already, get into God's Word and meditate upon it habitually. Read a verse or a chapter daily and digest the truth and let it speak to your heart consistently.

149 HEAR MY VOICE ACCORDING TO YOUR LOVINGKINDNESS; O LORD, REVIVE ME ACCORDING TO YOUR JUSTICE.

God is love. As we read the Bible, we come to comprehend the greatness of the Lord's love. We are comforted and consoled by the love of God to such an extent that every worldly discouragement fades away. The kindness of God, when integrated into our lives, changes a person from the inside out. Out of the Lord's love He revives the heart that is slumbering and complacent. God can jostle the dead heart and make it alive. God's Word has done so much refining in my own heart that it blows me away. I can't believe how much I've grown spiritually because of reading the Bible.

Ephesians 3:17-19 says, "That you, being rooted and grounded in love, may be able to comprehend with all the saints what is the width and length and depth and height—to know the love of Christ which passes knowledge; that you may be filled with all the fullness of God." This is what happens when I read through the Scriptures. I realize the vastness of God's love for me and it really puts life into perspective. Know that the Lord absolutely loves you. He is kind toward you and wants you to stay in line with His perfect will. He has a heart of compassion toward you that is unlike anything else in this world. Allow God to revive your heart daily and grow you to such an extent that your faith flourishes.

150 THEY DRAW NEAR WHO FOLLOW AFTER WICKEDNESS; THEY ARE FAR FROM YOUR LAW.

The wicked were drawing near to the psalmist. These guys were not adhering to God's Word, they were walking in the world's ways. They had no regard for the truth and no desire to do what was right in the Lord's eyes. They were far from the law of the Lord and they were chasing down those who believed in it.

We don't have to worry about the wicked because God is with us and fighting for us. I don't have to fear those who are against what I believe. I just simply relay the truth that I've been endowed with. We can thank God that we have His Word so that we know the truth and can walk in the light. The Bible is the compass that directs who we live for and how we live our lives. God's Word is rich and it leads us to worship the One who is devoid of darkness.

If you're reading this, then most likely you love God's Word and understand its major value in your life. The Bible says that you are protected on every side because the Lord is with you and for you. Every step you take is in the footsteps of the Lord who goes before you. Therefore, there is no reason to fear, doubt or worry. The hedge He has built around you is high enough to keep the darkness out.

151 YOU ARE NEAR, O LORD, AND ALL YOUR COMMANDMENTS ARE TRUTH.

Knowing God is near brings comfort like nothing else in this world. Sometimes we are so sure of God's promises and we believe without a shadow of a doubt that God is near. At other times, we feel like God is distant. It seems like He is far away and we're trying to reach Him. We must remember that if we feel far from God, it's not God who has moved. The best action to take when we feel distant from God is to get into His perfect Word. When we read the Bible, we are reminded of the Lord's location. He is with us wherever we go!

On occasion I live through dry seasons where I feel like I'm just going through the motions. I don't feel revival in my heart, I'm just trying to maintain. During those times I know I need to stay in God's Word, stay in prayer, and stay connected with other believers. Even during those dry desert seasons, we need to let the Word of God wash over us and instill His eternal promises to us. Take heart knowing that God will never leave you and He will never abandon you. His truth is what will take away the complacency that you may experience from time to time. He is near to you and He loves you so much.

152 CONCERNING YOUR TESTIMONIES, I HAVE KNOWN OF OLD THAT YOU HAVE FOUNDED THEM FOREVER.

God's Word testifies of who God is and what He's done. The Bible makes clear God's plans, prophecies and promises. It outlines how the Lord used men and women to advance His work and His kingdom. It is the blueprint for what we believe in and follow, the foundation on which our lives are built. We can know the Lord by reading and getting to know His Word. When we read and believe in what God says in His Word, our hearts begin to change and our eyes begin to open. We come to understand the heart of the Lord and we can, with the power of the Holy Spirit, emulate His heart. I love relaxing with a cup of coffee on a quiet morning and just reading the Bible. I love to pray it in and see and receive what God wants to speak to me. The Lord wants to speak to you as well. As your Bible is open, make sure your heart is also open to receive the Lord's leading in your life. God's testimonies can touch the parts of your heart that no one else can touch. The Bible will work in your life and situation when you get into it and stay in it.

153 CONSIDER MY AFFLICTION AND DELIVER ME, FOR I DO NOT FORGET YOUR LAW.

God knows what we face in this fallen world. Afflictions and hardships sometimes bombard us as believers. Storms enter our world and seem to keep beating down on us, causing torrents of rain. Physical, emotional, mental and spiritual battles surround us often. This is the exact reason we cannot forget God's law. If we only peer out into the world, we will be down and depressed. If we focus on the Scriptures, we can face every situation with a sure hope and confidence in Christ. The promises contained in the Word of God are what uplift us when we are down and out. They remind us that God is in charge. They get our eyes off the outward circumstances so we can focus on the blessings from above. Even if you are facing major trials right now, God is still with you and He will get you through. Read God's Word and don't forget the hope that He heralds into your very heart.

154 PLEAD MY CAUSE AND REDEEM ME; REVIVE ME ACCORDING TO YOUR WORD.

God fights for us. We don't have to worry about repercussions from living out our faith. The psalmist avidly sought help from God because He knew the heart of God. The Lord is our defender in any and every situation. We surrender and the Lord settles our hearts and sets up a hedge of protection around us. Not only does God defend us, He also revives us as we read the Scriptures. I can't tell you how many times I've read God's Word and my heart wakes up. My complacency dissolves as the Lord speaks to my heart and reminds me what life is all about. God's Word reverts my focus off of myself and onto the Lord. Don't hold back from seeking the Lord's help in prayer. It is never a negative action to get into His Word. God wants to revive your heart and instill in you a deep passion to follow His ways. Make it a daily spiritual habit to get into the Scriptures and allow the Lord to annihilate your apathy.

155 SALVATION IS FAR FROM THE WICKED, FOR THEY DO NOT SEEK YOUR STATUTES.

Salvation is far from the unsaved because they do not seek God's Word or God's ways. Yet, it's important to still have hope for lost souls. We are not called to give up on people and count them out of God's kingdom. Even if they claim to hate the faith, we can still love them and pray for them. We should never have that us-versus-them mentality. We were all created by God and He wants all to be saved. The fact is that some will accept, and some will reject. We are to do all we can to share the gospel with unbelievers, remembering that every person is a soul with the opportunity to be saved. I've talked to people who are just angry at God and I have had the privilege of relaying God's heart to them. It's a joy to spread the gospel in this godless world. May we see people as lost souls needing to be saved. Continue to pray for your unsaved friends and family, and when the Lord gives opportunities, step out in faith and share God's Word with them.

156 GREAT ARE YOUR TENDER MERCIES, O LORD; REVIVE ME ACCORDING TO YOUR JUDGMENTS.

We would not exist were it not for God's mercies. God giving us mercy means that the Lord does not give us what we deserve. We are innate sinners and we must repent in order to get right with the Lord. We've made many mistakes and we still have bouts of failure. But we can be forgiven, and this is why we can rejoice over God's great mercy toward us. The Bible makes it clear that even though we fall way short of God's standards, yet He still loves us and is growing us in grace and mercy. The Scriptures bring rejuvenation to our hearts and relief from the burden of our mistakes. I am so thankful that God's mercies are new every single day. Without His mercies I would not be here. I encourage you to get into God's Word and take in His mercies. Read what He has to say to you and watch as your heart gets revived. How amazing it is to walk with the Lord in this life.

157 MANY ARE MY PERSECUTORS AND MY ENEMIES, YET I DO NOT TURN FROM YOUR TESTIMONIES.

As Christians we have pressures that seem to surround us on a daily basis. Distractions threaten to steal us away from what truly matters in life. Conflicts cause chaos in our hearts as we attempt to stay afloat in a sinking and desperate world. Oppression can cause us to walk away from the faith and give up.

What is the key to standing firm in the midst of massive storms? God's Word. If we daily fill our hearts and minds with the Scriptures, we will stay on track. The moment we put off reading the Bible is the moment we cease to put on the armor of God. I don't ever want to turn from the Lord's testimonies. They are rich, powerful, and a protection against major life discouragement.

In my early Christian life, I was lured away into the things of the world. I procrastinated in reading the Bible. I quickly realized that God's Word is my lifeline. It is what I use as an offensive weapon on this ruthless earth—like Jesus did in defending Himself against the temptations of the devil. You can be protected on every side when you stay in the Scriptures and seek the Lord regularly. Use God's Word as a weapon against those unseen forces that work together to take you down. Stay in the Word and you'll get through this world with godly confidence and a fullness of joy.

158 I SEE THE TREACHEROUS, AND AM DISGUSTED, BECAUSE THEY DO NOT KEEP YOUR WORD.

The psalmist was taken aback seeing those who were disgracing God and His Word. We who follow the Lord know the absolute blessing of loving God and His Word. We've been saved and redeemed, and as we grow in Him our eyes are opened to His amazingness. Those who don't keep His precepts and even go against them cause our hearts turmoil. We want people to see the Lord and follow Him. We desire for the unsaved and the mockers to be moved by God and repent.

Sometimes I get angry at those who make fun of the faith and talk against me for what I believe. It bothers me when people use the Lord's name in vain and have no regard for the things of God. Yet, I am called to be a light to them and love them with the Lord's love.

You are called to be a light to those who reject the Lord, those who think God doesn't exist. You are commissioned to be a witness and share the truth with those who don't believe the truth. God will equip you to give a defense of the faith and give you courage to confront those who disbelieve.

159 CONSIDER HOW I LOVE YOUR PRECEPTS; REVIVE ME, O LORD, ACCORDING TO YOUR LOVINGKINDNESS.

God is pleased with those who are constantly reading His precepts. When we are in His Word, we gain insight into His heart and wisdom for life. One of the best prayers we can pray is that the Lord would revive us. There are times when we are slumbering spiritually. During those dim moments, we can cry out to God to get us up and get us going.

The psalmist makes it clear that God's love awakens a complacent heart. The Lord's love brings rejuvenation to the soul and revival to life. I've been in some low places in my life, but when I pondered the magnitude of the Lord's love for me, it always lifted me up. God's lovingkindness can lift your countenance. As you seek Him in prayer and through His Word, allow His love to overshadow the negative parts of your heart. Let His love flow into your heart and refresh your soul. Feed off of the Lord's faithfulness and keep going forward!

160 THE ENTIRETY OF YOUR WORD IS TRUTH, AND EVERY ONE OF YOUR RIGHTEOUS JUDGMENTS ENDURES FOREVER.

God's Word is complete. The canon of Scripture makes up the text that God has given to us. Not only is it complete, it is completely true. We do believe in absolute truth and the source of absolute truth is our almighty God. The Bible is not a book of questions to contemplate; it is a book of truth to believe in and act upon. It is not just a book of suggestions to flip through; it is a book of truth to adhere to. His Word is perfect and it works on my heart to refine me. God's Word is old but not outdated. I love that I have a blueprint for how to live my Christian life. God's Word isn't just a literary masterpiece that we read as a novel; it is divine.

As you dig into it, God's purposes become clear and you can accomplish them by His strength. His Word will endure in your heart and life. Dig into it and glean what God wants you to glean. Enjoy God's eternal Word. You will never stop growing spiritually as long as you are in the Word of God.

161 PRINCES PERSECUTE ME WITHOUT A CAUSE, BUT MY HEART STANDS IN AWE OF YOUR WORD.

Opposition is not a reason to back down from what we believe in. When our hearts and lives are established on God's eternal Word, nothing will move us away from that foundation. People may fling accusatory statements at us, they may mock our faith, they may criticize the faithful actions we take, yet we will not back down. When we understand the greatness of God's Word, we will stand in awe of the Lord who breathed the Word into existence.

From the time I became a new believer until now, I have been enamored and amazed at God's Word. The Scriptures speak to my heart as I sink my eyes into the pages and soak in God's absolute truth into my life. I am hungry for truth and the answers to life's questions are in the testimonies of the Lord. You have the opportunity to daily invest in eternal matters. You can read God's Word, soak it in, and realize how beautiful the Bible actually is. Do not ever let opposition or persecution stop you from being on fire for God. "So because we stand in awe of the one true Lord, we make it our aim to convince all people of the truth of the gospel" (2 Corinthians 5:11 Voice).

162 I REJOICE AT YOUR WORD AS ONE WHO FINDS GREAT TREASURE.

True treasure emanates from the Word, not from the world. So many people strive their whole lives to gain what will never make them happy. Material possessions are a desire that does not fulfill or satisfy the heart. Relationships will not bring permanent everyday happiness to our lives either. The treasure that can turn our hearts from being in want to being satisfied is God's Word. The Scriptures are riches that we all can have and grow spiritually rich from. We can rejoice because the Lord has given us His Word to enjoy and direct us.

I absolutely love digging into the treasure trove that is the Scriptures. God speaks to me through His Word. I encourage you to make a daily spiritual habit of digging into the riches of God's Word. You'll be amazed at how the Lord speaks to your heart and refines your life. The direction that you are seeking can be found in the faithful truths in Scripture. Get into the treasure that is the Bible and hear God speak to you and direct your life according to His will.

163 I HATE AND ABHOR LYING, BUT I LOVE YOUR LAW.

As we grow in faith through God's Word, we come to hate sin. When sin looks good, it threatens to lure us away from our Lord. Sin never looks nasty on the outside. But when we partake of it, we see how ugly it is. May we grow to love God's Word so much that we despise sin and forsake those habitual sins that can ensnare us. When we fall in love with our almighty God, we will grow to abhor the ways of the world.

I find that when I'm consistently in the Scriptures, my daily desire is to follow after the Lord and forsake sin. When I'm not in the Scriptures, that's when I'm most susceptible to making ungodly decisions and stumbling into sin. Fall in love with God's Word and read it daily. Feed your soul constantly so that your desire to sin will be crowded out and replaced with a desire to serve the Lord.

FALLING IN LOVE WITH GOD'S WORD

164 SEVEN TIMES A DAY I PRAISE YOU, BECAUSE OF YOUR RIGHTEOUS JUDGMENTS.

Continual praise to God makes for a heightened countenance. Our God is worthy to be praised every day, all day. He has done more for us than any human being can or will ever do. What a blessing to pour our hearts out to the God who gave us life and then saved our souls! We can worship the Lord because He is just and loving at the same time. As we peer into His precepts, one of the things we read over and over again is that God is slow to anger. He isn't waiting there for someone to mess up so He can strike them down with lightning. He is full of love and grace. God is and will be forever fair. The more I read through the Word of God, the more I realize how righteous and merciful God is. I want to keep growing and flourishing in the faith, and the source of growth is the Scriptures. If you want to get to know God's heart, get into the Bible on a regular basis. The more you read and pray in God's precepts, the clearer your view of God will be. The result of daily digging into the Bible will be joyful praise.

165 GREAT PEACE HAVE THOSE WHO LOVE YOUR LAW, AND NOTHING CAUSES THEM TO STUMBLE.

The Scriptures bring peace and perseverance to the hearts of those who believe. During those stressed-out moments, we can get into the Scriptures for direction and peace. At times we feel so out of control and unsure. Many times we feel anxious and nervous. We struggle with chaotic thoughts that run through our minds. Realistically, life can seem so crazy. Thank the Lord that we have His Word to bring peace to our hearts and stability to our minds. There have been countless times where I have had no peace about a situation in my life and it majorly stressed me out. But when I opened His living Word, it seriously calmed my mind and spoke to my heart. The Lord is faithful to pacify the chaos in my life by speaking to me through the Scriptures. When you are stressed out and filled with unrest, get into God's Word and peace will flood into your soul. God's Word will keep you grounded and levelheaded. You will persevere as you rest upon the statutes of the Lord. You will make it through with a settled heart as you consistently stay in the Scriptures.

166 LORD, I HOPE FOR YOUR SALVATION, AND I DO YOUR COMMANDMENTS.

Saved, forgiven and free—this is a sure future for those who believe in and follow Jesus. When we think about how the Lord has pulled us out of the pit of despair, we are amazed and awestruck. God has saved us from death, darkness and destruction. Our response to such love should be willing obedience to the One who set us free. I'll never forget an action of a believer I used to know. At every prayer meeting, he would start his prayers saying, "Thank You, Lord, for my salvation." Honestly, it always reminded me how blessed I am to be saved. It's beautiful how God changed my heart and renewed my mind. I can barely handle how good God has been and is to me. I pray that you are reminded how blessed you are to be saved. I pray that you would revel in the goodness and grace of God. I pray that as a result of realizing His blessings, you'd get into God's Word and let the Lord continue to direct your life.

"By the mercies of God … present your bodies a living sacrifice, holy, acceptable to God, which is your reasonable service. And do not be conformed to this world, but be transformed by the renewing of your mind, that you may prove what is that good and acceptable and perfect will of God" (Romans 12:1-2).

167 MY SOUL KEEPS YOUR TESTIMONIES, AND I LOVE THEM EXCEEDINGLY.

Our soul is fed by the faithful Word of God. What we put into our soul matters for our spiritual health. If we feed off of the carnality of the world, our soul will be corrupted and skewed. If we feed off of the things of God, our soul will be nourished and healthy. When we partake of the Scriptures and digest the decrees of the Lord, we will be built up in the faith.

I want a spiritual life that is thriving and constantly moving forward. I want a faith that doesn't falter or fall to the ground. I want to live fully for the Lord on a daily basis. I've found that as I read the Word of God, all of these things actually happen! If I keep digging into the Word I'll keep growing as a Christian. There have been seasons in my life where I wasn't consistent in reading the Bible and I definitely struggled through those seasons. But the times where I was consistently in God's Word, no matter what happened externally, internally I was established in the faith and grounded in God's Word.

You will continue to grow and flourish as you daily read the Bible. The more you read, the more you'll fall in love with what God has written. Nourish your soul with the Scriptures and lean upon God's Word for every aspect of your life.

168 I KEEP YOUR PRECEPTS AND YOUR TESTIMONIES, FOR ALL MY WAYS ARE BEFORE YOU.

When we hold fast to the precepts of the Lord, we will be walking in the center of God's will. Apart from the Lord, our ways are not going to lead to our divine destination. The ways of the Lord are amazing, His plan is perfect. Our calling in life is to seek the Lord for His will for us, and then live out His will. We can lay out our plans before the Lord and allow Him to prioritize and make clear what He wants us to do and where He wants us to go.

Sometimes the plans I have seem like a great idea to me, so I implement them. I quickly realize my ideas were not close to being aligned with the Lord's plans. I have to depend upon God to guide me and lead the way because that's always the best action to take! As you plan for the future, make sure you seek the Lord for His divine direction. Study His precepts and never doubt that He has amazing plans for you!

169 LET MY CRY COME BEFORE YOU, O LORD; GIVE ME UNDERSTANDING ACCORDING TO YOUR WORD.

When we fall upon the Word of God in dependence, we gain understanding for life. We all struggle and deal with difficulties that are sometimes too intense and deep. There will always be pressures to deal with. As a result, we can end up discouraged and even broken. We can feel defeated and deflated. How should we respond to such hardships? Pray to the One who understands and cares. The Lord knows what we are going through and He already knew we would be going through them. We have pure wisdom available to us whenever we want. God's Word is the wisdom that we need to navigate through this life.

Time and time again I would go through trials that seem unending and incredibly tough. Problems can be compounded and complicated. Yet, when I seek the Lord through His Word, the answers become clear. The Word gives me wisdom to deal with the toughest trials. Cry before the Lord and according to His Word, He will open your eyes, comfort your heart, and give you understanding.

170 LET MY SUPPLICATION COME BEFORE YOU; DELIVER ME ACCORDING TO YOUR WORD.

Prayer and the Word are an unstoppable combination. We need to depend upon the Lord for deliverance in this life. Yes, for salvation, but also from those deep discouraging moments that we face. In order to dig us out of the hole we find ourselves in, we have to pray for God to pull us out! He will deliver us from drowning and He will draw near to us as we continually seek Him. Deliverance only comes through Jesus Christ.

I didn't know anything about the Bible until I began reading it on my own. I wasn't a believer but as I read, the truth was revealed to me; I was delivered and saved.

I had new life. Don't forget where deliverance comes from. God is the One who has and will continue to deliver you in this life. Look to Him often. Seek Him always. Know that His Word makes it clear He has you!

171 MY LIPS SHALL UTTER PRAISE, FOR YOU TEACH ME YOUR STATUTES.

When worship and the Word are cohesive, we will grow in the Lord exponentially. We praise God because He is so good. We know God is so good because we learn of Him in His Word. As we daily get into the Scriptures, our hearts will overflow into a natural response of worship. We are blessed that we get to praise God and learn of His precepts. I am enamored and in awe at my amazing God. The more I read His Word, the more I want to worship God with my entire life. He is so good in every situation and through all of my circumstances. The Scriptures are the avenue for you to see who God is and to praise Him as a result. As you remain teachable, the Lord will fill you to overflowing with His truth. The amazing result will be a heart of praise and a life of adoration.

172 MY TONGUE SHALL SPEAK OF YOUR WORD, FOR ALL YOUR COMMANDMENTS ARE RIGHTEOUSNESS.

We are privileged to take the Word in and to give the Word out. As Christians we are messengers. We are ambassadors for the Lord and deliverers of the gospel. We get recharged as we study the Scriptures and then we get to go out and share the truths we've learned. It is a blessing to speak God's Word to those who don't know it. Some think it's a burden to share the gospel with those in this lost world. If I overthink a possible conversation I may have with an unbeliever about things of God, I will usually be nervous and freeze up. But if I pray that the Holy Spirit would lead me, He always comes through and the conversation is led of God. The more I share the gospel with people, the bolder I become to share the gospel. My courage increases when I consistently talk to others about the Lord. As you daily read God's Word, take what you've learned and tell others. You'll find it's not a burden but an absolute blessing. God's Word relayed will accomplish God's will on this earth.

"Praise the Lord, call upon His name; declare His deeds among the peoples, make mention that His name is exalted" (Isaiah 12:4).

173 LET YOUR HAND BECOME MY HELP, FOR I HAVE CHOSEN YOUR PRECEPTS.

God is our help and His law directs our lives. Those moments when we feel lost and struggle immensely, we have to remember the Lord is our help. Counselors, friends, and even our spouse are great sources to seek; yet, the Lord our God is who we should seek first in all conflicted circumstances (Matthew 6:33). He is our help. I've gone through some intense and depressing events in my life; times where I've dug myself into a discouraging pit of despair. I've let life's troubles get to me and because of it, I had become sorrowful and nothing seemed good. In those times I've learned that the only way to get out of the miry clay of difficulties is to reach up to my God. Every single time He pulls me up and out and gets me moving forward in life. Choose His Word as the source of wisdom for life. Choose His Word to bring an encouraging truth that you can hold on to and use to lift you out of the pit of despair. Seek the Lord so you don't get stuck in a rut as you navigate through this life. You'll quickly realize that God truly is your help in times of trouble. "God is our refuge and strength, a very present help in trouble" (Psalm 46:1).

174 I LONG FOR YOUR SALVATION, O LORD, AND YOUR LAW IS MY DELIGHT.

We will be determined in what we delight in. When I think of my salvation, it blows me away. I cannot believe the Lord pursued me and saved my soul. That fact is astounding. Not only are we spiritually saved but in the heat of spiritual battle, the Lord comes through as well. No matter what we face, we can be sure that the Lord will carry us through in every season and stage of our lives. He is our rescuer, our deliverer, and our hope through heartache. It's okay to long for His salvation from situation to situation. God will get you through as you delight in His Word and depend upon Him. If you are going through the fire of affliction right now, take heart and know that God is with you and God will get you through. Delight in His words even during those dark times. He loves you and He will deliver you.

175 LET MY SOUL LIVE, AND IT SHALL PRAISE YOU; AND LET YOUR JUDGMENTS HELP ME.

We feed our souls with the Scriptures and it results in our souls crying out to our Savior. As we soak in the Scripture, we will respond to the Lord in worship. The Lord is so incredibly faithful to help us in life. He lifts us up when we are down and out, He forgives us when we fail, He gives us strength when we are weak. God always comes through and is forever faithful. As a response to His love and goodness, we cry out in praise to Him from our hearts.

I become overwhelmed when I think about all that God has done for me. It's almost too much to even consider God's goodness toward me. All I can do in this fallen world is praise the Lord who is faithful every day. If God has saved your soul, then set your mind upon Him and worship the Lord! He has blessed you already and desires that you respond to Him with your whole life. You will not regret it.

176 I HAVE GONE ASTRAY LIKE A LOST SHEEP; SEEK YOUR SERVANT, FOR I DO NOT FORGET YOUR COMMANDMENTS.

If we part from the Scriptures, we will go astray. The psalmist ends Psalm 119 not with pride for seeking to obey God's Word, but with humility realizing that without the Father, he is frail. He hasn't become self-righteous or holier than thou because of his faithfulness to the Scriptures. Rather, he is humbled by who God is knowing that without the Lord, he is nothing. God is our sufficiency and we look to Him in full dependence. He picks us up and leads us forward in this life. He loves us despite ourselves. He works to refine our lives and He knocks off those rough edges that threaten to lure us away from Him.

I am overly grateful at how good God is to me. I am overwhelmed by His love and enamored by His grace. I am so imperfect but I have the privilege of following my perfect God who paves the path for my very life. You are blessed. You serve a God who has given you His perfect Word to guide you and speak to your heart. As a believer you are compared to sheep and the Lord is your Good Shepherd. He leads you every step that you take in every type of terrain that you'll face. There's no need for you to worry for your Father knows what you need, what you are going through, and where you need to go. Trust in Him as you read His Word. Allow Him to speak and be completely amazed!

CONCLUSION

My prayer is that you'd get into God's Word and stay in God's Word. The Bible is the key to your spiritual growth. When you and I stay consistently grounded in the Scriptures, we will be able to face any situation with confidence and calm hearts. Allow the Scriptures to sink deep into your soul, alter your attitude, and give you a godly perspective for this life. Let the truth of the Bible mold your mind and guide your life. Fall in love with God's Word and you'll realize how in love the Lord is with you. God bless you in your walk with the Lord!

www.ingramcontent.com/pod-product-compliance
Lightning Source LLC
Chambersburg PA
CBHW060325050426
42449CB00011B/2659